# Transform
## Your Pastoral
## Ministry

# DAG HEWARD-MILLS

*Parchment House*

First published by Parchment House 2001
Published by Lux Verbi.BM (Pty) Ltd. 2008
Published by Parchment House 2011
9th Printing 2014

Find out more about Dag Heward-Mills
Healing Jesus Crusade
Write to: evangelist@daghewardmills.org
Website: www.daghewardmills.org
Facebook: Dag Heward-Mills
Twitter: @EvangelistDag

ISBN: 978-9988-596-46-0

Dedication
To
*Rev. Eddy Addy*
Thank you for your loyalty and friendship
through the years.

# Contents

1.  Why You Should Avoid a Pseudo Ministry......................1

2.  How You Can Achieve Excellence in Ministry................7

3.  Ten Reasons Why Every Minister Should Pray.............10

4.  Eighteen Facts about Spiritual Warfare...........................23

5.  Twenty Ways to Know Your Enemy so You Can
    Defeat Him..................................................................30

6.  Five Ways for Pastors to Pray Effectively.......................39

7.  Six Reasons for Praying Strategic Bible Prayers...........42

8.  Seven Examples of Praying Fervently............................47

9.  Seven Signs of Fervent Prayer.......................................52

10. Nine Steps to Praying for a Long Time..........................55

11. Two Steps to Understanding Intercession......................60

12. Twenty Reasons Why Every Pastor Needs an
    Intercessor.................................................................62

13. How to Intercede against the Law of Degeneration........65

14. How to Intercede against the Law of the World.............67

15. How to Intercede against the Law of the Flesh.............68

16. How to Intercede against the Law of the Elements.........70

17. How to Intercede against the Law of Humanity.............71

18. How to Intercede against the Law of Nature..................74

19. How to Intercede against the Law of the Devil...............76

20. How to Intercede against the Law of Time.....................78

21. How to Intercede against the Law of Creeping Things........................................................80

22. How to Intercede against the Law of Things Determined.....................................................82

23. How to Intercede against the Law of the Stars ...............84

24. How to Intercede about the Laws of God ......................86

25. Seven Signs That Show That You Are Engaged in Travailing Prayer...........................................88

26. Thirty-two Reasons Why I Pray in Tongues ..................91

27. Twelve Reasons Why Pastors Must Visit Their Sheep.............................................................95

28. Three Secrets behind the Power of Visitation................98

29. Eight Guidelines for Fruitful Visitation ........................100

30. Ten Rules for Visitation................................................102

31. Seven Tips That Make Visitation Easier ......................106

32. Five Visits That Have Life-Changing Power ................108

33. Five Visits That Bring a Permanent Change .................111

34. Five Visits That Establish Church Members.................115

35. Fifteen Keys to Becoming a Successful Teacher of the Word .....................................................119

36. Four Reasons Why Every Pastor Should See the Congregation as God's Garden ....................................124

37. Seven Reasons Why a Pastor Should Teach in Series............................................................127

38. Four Keys to Augment Your Teaching Ministry ...........129

39. Seven Reasons Why Listening to Tapes Will Transform Your Preaching Ministry..............................130

40. How to Establish a Doctrine in the Church....................132

41. Nine Reasons Why Pastors Should Preach
    the Word of God...........................................................134

42. Seven Reasons Why You Should Teach Your
    Leaders ........................................................................140

43. Why You Must Avoid "Pseudo Word" and
    Doctrines of Devils .....................................................142

44. Eight Reasons Why Interaction Is Important
    for Every Church...........................................................145

45. How to Interact with People...........................................148

46. Eight Ways You Can Make  People Feel Special..........150

47. How to Encourage Interaction between
    Church Members...........................................................153

48. P.V.T.I. .........................................................................155

# Part I

# REAL MINISTRY

*Chapter 1*

# Why You Should Avoid a Pseudo Ministry

In the Old Testament, true ministry was typified by the gold in the temple. Every important object in the temple was covered with pure gold. The Lord gave the design of the temple to Moses.

> And the Lord spake unto Moses, saying, Speak unto the children of Israel, that they bring me an offering... And let them make me a sanctuary; that I may dwell among them... And thou shalt make a mercy seat of pure gold... And thou shalt put the mercy seat above upon the ark; and in the ark thou shalt put the testimony that I shall give thee. And there I will meet with thee, and I will commune with thee from above the mercy seat...
>
> Exodus 25: 1,2,8,17,21,22

This is what God wanted His temple to look like. No man has the right to introduce his own variations into God's master plan. When King Solomon built the temple, he followed God's plan to the letter.

> And the oracle in the forepart was twenty cubits in length, and twenty cubits in breadth, and twenty cubits in the height thereof: and he overlaid it with pure GOLD; and so covered the altar which was of cedar. So Solomon overlaid the house within with PURE GOLD: and he made a partition by the chains of GOLD before the oracle; and he overlaid it with GOLD. And the whole house he overlaid with GOLD, until he had finished all the house: also the whole altar that was by the oracle he overlaid with GOLD... And within the oracle he made two cherubim of olive tree, each ten cubits high... And he overlaid the cherubim with GOLD... And the floor of the house he overlaid with GOLD, within and without.
>
> 1 Kings 6:20-23, 28,30

And Solomon made all the vessels that pertained unto the house of the Lord: the altar of GOLD, and the table of GOLD, whereupon the shewbread was, And the candlesticks of pure GOLD, five on the right side, and five on the left, before the oracle, with the flowers, and the lamps, and the tongs of GOLD, And the bowls, and the snuffers, and the basons, and the spoons, and the censers of pure GOLD; and the hinges of GOLD both for the doors of the inner house, the most holy place, and for the doors of the house, to wit, of the temple.

1 Kings 7:48-50

Many years later, another king substituted the gold with brass. Brass looks very much like gold. It is "close and parallel", but it is not gold. King Rehoboam brought brass into the Lord's house. It may have looked like the real thing but God was not pleased with it. Brass is an alloy consisting of copper and zinc. In reality, brass is very different from pure gold! Many people are deceived when the real is substituted for the pseudo. That is why I am writing this book.

So Shishak king of Egypt came up against Jerusalem, and took away the TREASURES of the house of the Lord and the treasures of the king's house; he took all: he carried away also the shields of gold which Solomon had made. Instead of which king Rehoboam made shields of BRASS, and committed them to the hands of the chief of the guard, that kept the entrance of the king's house.

2 Chronicles 12:9-10

Through this book, I want to help you to keep the gold in the temple. You must not substitute anything for real biblical ministry. As is the case with many professions, lay people do not really know what the professional does. Lay people do not really know, for example, what a pilot or doctor knows. It is important for everyone who is getting into the ministry to know what it is all about!

I realise that many people like to create a mystical air about what they do. They do this to enhance their image within the profession. However, the Lord has urged me to teach you what a pastor's real duties are. In this book, I will not attempt to cover every detail of a pastor's work. I am only going to share the main things with you.

It is my prayer that you will believe in the simplicity of the ministry. I realise that people often prefer complicated doctrines to simple truths. They feel that the more complicated the message is, the more likely it is from God. But the greatest truths are often simple enough for the common man to grasp.

In the Book of Acts, Peter and the other apostles arrived at a crossroad of ministry. At that crossroad, they had to decide which direction to take. **They had to decide whether they were going to be real ministers or secular administrators.** But they chose real ministry!

Then the twelve called the multitude of the disciples unto them, and said, It is not reason that we should LEAVE THE WORD OF GOD, AND SERVE TABLES. Wherefore, brethren, look ye out among you seven men of honest report, full of the Holy Ghost and wisdom, whom we may appoint over this business. But WE WILL GIVE OURSELVES CONTINUALLY TO PRAYER, AND TO THE MINISTRY OF THE WORD.

Acts 6:2-4

You must be able to differentiate between *true ministry* and *pseudo-ministry*. A pseudo-ministry is not the real thing! Like brass, which is a poor substitute for gold, it is close and parallel to the real thing. There are many things that look like true ministry, but are not.

For instance, being a church administrator makes you busy around the ministry. Many pastors are actually administrators. They are seen to be busy in and around the church office. Psychologically, they feel that they are working for God. After all, the rest of the world is in offices and behind computers. People seem to have something important to do from nine to five every day. They go out there as secretaries, security men, computer programmers and so on. If the pastor is not seen to

3

be doing something similar, he feels unemployed. I have had people ring me at home at eleven o'clock in the morning. They would ask if I were still asleep. They assume that a pastor sleeps all week.

Dear ministers of the Gospel, do not be moved by people's opinions. Do not yield to worldly pressures. It is the prince of the power of the air who governs and directs the world. Everything in the world is controlled from the Spirit realm. Satan is a clever being and has deceived the whole world. But this deception must not come into the church.

**Wherein in time past ye walked according to the course of this world, according to the prince of the power of the air, the spirit that now worketh in the children of disobedience:**

**Ephesians 2:2**

The world has been deceived into thinking that there is no life after death. "Eat, drink and be merry for tomorrow we die! When you die you are dead like a dog! Heaven is on earth and hell is on earth! Life is what you make it!" These subtle slogans have influenced the masses to live their lives chasing after money and pleasure.

When this kind of thinking enters the church, people feel that only secular (non-spiritual) things are of importance. Even pastors are under pressure to buy computers and sit in offices like everyone else. But we are not "everyone else"! We are shepherds of God's flock!

Shepherds are "dirty" people who live among the sheep. Shepherds are people who give their lives for the sheep. A shepherd is not an armchair executive!

When you declare that your work is prayer, you immediately look queer! Government officials have the audacity to suggest that the church spend its time doing more "fruitful" things. Indeed! What is more fruitful than prayer? Why should we listen to unbelievers tell us how to do our job? Why should godless men teach the church her duties?

The church has come under so much pressure that many ministers have set aside the Great Commission. The Great Commission is our principal instruction from the head of the church.

**Go ye therefore, and teach all nations, baptizing them in the name of the Father, and of the Son, and of the Holy Ghost: Teaching them to observe all things whatsoever I have commanded you: and, lo, I am with you always even unto the end of the world. Amen.**

**Matthew 28:19,20**

Read it for yourself! It is in black and white! There is no mention of social, health or educational work. **Health and education may be by-products of the Great Commission but a by-product must not become the main product!**

Today, large sections of the church are mere hospitals, schools, relief organisations and social clubs. This is unfortunate! You will notice that secular health organisations and educational institutions do not set aside their jobs to preach the Word of God! Satan smiles approvingly as the ministers of the Gospel metamorphose into politicians, social workers and health workers. The gold of ministry has been substituted with brass!

This attitude filters down to the ordinary Christian. One day, a young student brought me a report from the university.

He said, "Pastor, God is moving on the campus!"

I said, "Really, what is happening?"

He said, "God is working!"

So I asked, "How is God moving? What is He doing?"

He said to me, "People are passing their exams!"

I was taken aback. *"Exams?"*

Although I didn't voice it out, I thought to myself, "When God moves, people get saved and filled with the Spirit." Passing exams is a blessing from God but it is not the *move of God.* Let

5

us not get confused about God's work. Let us understand what the Bible teaches about ministry. Let's not mistake brass for gold. Let us avoid the judgement of Rehoboam by bringing only gold into the temple.

It is my prayer that as you read this book you will understand what pastors, shepherds and church leaders are supposed to do. It's time to move away from "pseudo-ministry". We cannot hasten the return of the Lord Jesus Christ with something that looks like the real thing but is not.

# Three Reasons

In summary, these are the three reasons why we should avoid a pseudo ministry:

1.  **The church is the only institution that is mandated to preach the Gospel and make disciples of every nation.** No one else will do our job for us!

2.  **We must not try to impress the world by doing things that they want us to do.** God is the one who called us and He is the one we must seek to please.

3.  **We can only defeat Satan and his cohorts with real ministry!** A pseudo ministry has no place in this great end-time battle.

I have a little code that will help you and I to remember the humble duties of a God ordained pastor. And it goes like this: **P** for prayer, **V** for visitation, **T** for teaching (counselling and preaching) and **I** for interaction. (P.V.T.I.)

*Chapter 2*

# How You Can Achieve Excellence in Ministry

You can achieve excellence in ministry! Your ministry does not have to be mediocre. However, you must realize that excellence must be achieved by *God's standards*, and not *human standards*. In this short chapter, I want to show you four keys that brought excellence to Jesus' ministry.

Jesus Christ is the greatest example for all of us. He is given to us so we can see what God looks like. In every situation we have the best example to follow.

**Who being the brightness of his glory, and the EXPRESS IMAGE of his person...**
**Hebrews 1:3**

Remember this! When you don't know what to do, do what Jesus did. Jesus is the good shepherd (John 10:11). He is the best example of a pastor you could ever have. Are you a good pastor? Who endorses your ministry—God or man? Would Jesus say "Well done, good and faithful servant" to you?

## Jesus the Model of Excellence

Since Jesus is the example of excellence, let us look at Jesus for direction in ministry. I want us to look at four main areas of the good Shepherd's ministry: prayer, visitation, teaching and interaction (PVTI). A good understanding of these four aspects of Jesus' ministry will transform your pastoral ministry.

### 1. Prayer

And in the morning, rising up a great while before day, he went out, and departed into a solitary place, and there PRAYED.

Mark 1:35

## 2.   Visitation

And forthwith, when they were come out of the synagogue, they ENTERED INTO THE HOUSE of Simon and Andrew, with James and John...

Mark 1:29-31

## 3.   Teaching

And he said unto them, Let us go into the next towns, that I may PREACH there also: for therefore came I forth. And he PREACHED in their synagogues throughout all Galilee, and cast out devils.

Mark 1:38,39

## 4.   Interaction

Now as HE WALKED BY THE SEA OF GALILEE, HE SAW SIMON AND ANDREW his brother casting a net into the sea: for they were fishers. And JESUS SAID UNTO THEM, Come ye after me, and I will make you to become fishers of men.

Mark 1:16,17

These Scriptures show us that Jesus was a man of prayer, a man of preaching, a man of visitation and a man who interacted with the people.

# Part II

# PRAYER

## Chapter 3

# Ten Reasons Why
# Every Minister Should Pray

Prayer is the foundation for every real ministry. Prayer is actually *the ministry*. Anyone who discovers this reality will have a great and fruitful ministry. Let me give you ten reasons why every minister should pray.

## The Ten Reasons

### 1. Pray because prayer is a great act of faith.

Prayer is one of the greatest acts of faith. I never used to think so! I always used to think that praying was different from exercising faith. **But now I realise that prayer demonstrates and releases faith**. The reason for this is simple; whenever you pray, you are declaring that you do not have faith in the arm of flesh. Have you not noticed that every time you begin to pray, one hundred different "things to do" come to your mind?

Something tells you to make a call. Something says to you 'get up and go'. Something tells you to organise that meeting so that you have good success. When you decide to pray, you are saying that prayer will have a greater effect than all those physical things you have to do. In other words, you are saying that God's direct intervention is the most important thing for your ministry. That is faith in the arm of God.

**And he spake a parable unto them to this end, that men ought always to pray, and not to faint; Saying, There was in a city a judge, which feared not God, neither regarded man: And there was a widow in that city; and she came unto him, saying, Avenge me of mine adversary. And he would not for a while: but afterward he said within himself, Though I fear not God, nor regard man; Yet because this widow troubleth me, I**

**will avenge her, lest by her continual coming she weary me. And the Lord said, Hear what the unjust judge saith. And shall not God avenge his own elect, which cry day and night unto him, though he bear long with them? I tell you that he will avenge them speedily. Nevertheless when the Son of man cometh, SHALL HE FIND FAITH on the earth?**

**Luke 18:1-8**

After this great lesson on prayer, Jesus asked an important question. Will I find faith on earth? He was asking: 'will I find people on earth who pray?' In other words, Jesus wondered whether He would find this expression of faith (prayer) when He returned to the earth.

## Prayer Is an Expression of Faith

Do you want to be a great man of faith? A man of faith is a man of great exploits. Become a great man of faith by becoming a man of prayer. Prayer is one of the greatest expressions of faith in God.

**But without faith it is impossible to please him: for he that cometh to God must believe that he is, and that he is a rewarder of them that diligently seek him.**

**Hebrews 11:6**

As you can see, you cannot please God without faith. That means you cannot please God in the ministry without prayer. You do not please God by being an administrator, accountant or computer wizard. You please God by praying and demonstrating faith in Him.

2.  **Pray because prayer makes you into a man of authority.**

**And it came to pass, when Jesus had ended these sayings, the people were astonished at his doctrine: For he taught them AS ONE HAVING AUTHORITY, and not as the scribes.**

**Matthew 7:28,29**

You will notice that Jesus was a man of authority. Authority can be explained as the *"not-easily-defined, invisible, magnetic aura that surrounds a man of God."* Authority emanates from your closeness to God. The closer you are to a person, the more confidently you speak about him. You will have more authority when you speak of him.

For instance, when a great man dies, his death may not be announced immediately. There are different reasons for this. For instance, one of the heads of state of Nigeria, General Aguiyi-Ironsi, was assassinated on the 28th July 1966, but it was not announced until 14th January 1967. However, if you were close to the family you would have been able to speak authoritatively about whether he was dead or alive. If you said that the person was dead, people would believe you because of your closeness. *The closer you are, the more authority you have.*

The more you pray the closer you are to God. If you are close to God it means you have more authority with God and with man. As you pray people will not be able to explain that invisible magnetic aura that surrounds you. You will have a following without even understanding why people follow you! You will have a crowd without being able to explain why! Your teaching will have more power! Your instructions will be obeyed! All these are the results of ministerial prayer that make you into a man of authority.

## How Jesus Became a Man of Authority

Jesus was not introduced to this world by anyone. He was not appointed as a teacher by anyone. In fact, His background was questioned and many had reservations about his parentage. But Jesus knew the secret of having authority with man. He went into the wilderness and waited on God.

**And Jesus returned in the power of the Spirit into Galilee: and there went out a fame of him through all the region round about.**

**Luke 4:14**

The word "power" is translated from the Greek word *dunamis.* *Dunamis* means *"miraculous power, ability, abundance, strength, violence, mighty wonderful work and enabling power."* Jesus had become a man of authority! He had new strength, abundance and power. This new invisible magnetic aura around Jesus was derived from prayer. The response to his first sermon in Nazareth was amazing.

**AND ALL BEAR HIM WITNESS AND WONDERED at the gracious words which proceeded out of his mouth.**

**Luke 4:22**

Jesus had equally great results in Capernaum. People were simply amazed with his preaching and ministry.

**And came down to Capernaum, a city of Galilee, and taught them on the sabbath days. AND THEY WERE ASTONISHED at his doctrine: for his word was with power.**

**Luke 4:31,32**

Where do you think this authority and success came from? Where did all these crowds come from? Why were people suddenly listening to this thirty-year-old man? This is what I call the *"not-easily-defined, invisible, magnetic aura that surrounds a man of prayer."* Perhaps you don't have anyone to introduce you in ministry. Like Jesus, you can become a man of authority and receive recognition.

### 3. Pray because prayer makes you a man of anointing.

When you are close to someone, something rubs off on you. Whenever you spend time in prayer, you are spending time talking to God. The more you talk to someone, the closer you become to the person. The closer you are to someone, the more things rub off on you. Do you want some of God's glory to be on you? Do you want the anointing to be on your life?

I wish I could offer you an easier way but only prayer will bring you close to God.

The example of Moses tells it all. Moses went into the mountain and stayed in the presence of the Lord for a long time.

**And Moses went into the midst of the cloud, and gat him up into the mount: and Moses was in the mount forty days and forty nights.**

**Exodus 24:18**

You will notice that Moses was a man who spent long hours with the Lord. After being so long on the mountain, the glory of the Lord was evident on him. Dear pastor, this is what will happen to you when you spend hours with the Lord. There will be glory on your life and ministry.

**But if the ministration of death written and engraven in stones, was glorious, so that the children of Israel could not stedfastly behold THE FACE OF MOSES FOR THE GLORY of his countenance...**

**2 Corinthians 3:7**

## 4. Pray because prayer binds demonic activities in your ministry.

Dear pastor friend, a church is not a secular organisation. You need to bind the devil for several important reasons:

a. You must bind his activity that causes divisions and disloyalty amongst leaders.

b. You must bind his influence that causes backsliding, immorality and sin in your members.

c. You must bind the demons that cause poverty, depression and oppression in your members.

d. You must bind the spirits that raise accusations and slander against the church.

Whether you like it or not, Satan assigns demons to attack and destroy the church. I suggest you read my book, *Leaders and Loyalty* to get a fuller revelation of the activity of demons against your ministry.

**If you do not bind the devil he will bind you in your own church.** You will be unable to minister. No one will receive from you and you will wonder what is going on. The devil will scatter your congregation time and time again. There will be a complex network of stories, accusations, slander and discussions that constantly divide the church. Rise up today and bind Satan and demons in your church.

5. **Pray because prayer creates and gives birth to new dimensions in ministry.**

   **...for as soon as Zion travailed, SHE BROUGHT FORTH HER CHILDREN.**
   **Isaiah 66:8**

   A very important revelation about prayer is the fact that prayer has a creative potential. If you are starting out in ministry, you will need to pray until something that doesn't exist comes into existence. Creating something is different from maintaining it.

   Many people can maintain what has been created but it takes a man of prayer to create new things.

   If you are sent out to do a pioneering work, be a man of prayer. A man of prayer is a man who creates new spiritual dimensions. The Apostle Paul was a man of prayer. He said,

   **My little children, of whom I travail in birth again until CHRIST BE FORMED IN YOU.**
   **Galatians 4:19**

   Paul had to travail for Christ to be formed in these Christians. Paul did not try to do it by any other means. **Forming committees, organising meetings, having Bible studies and showing love does not create new dimensions.** I have been involved in establishing new churches, fellowships and ministries for many years. From my experience I can give you a little suggestion.

The first suggestion is, PRAY. The second suggestion is also to PRAY. And the third is to PRAY!

## 6. Pray because prayer is the first apostolic command to every minister.

The apostle Paul had a lot of good advice and teaching for his son Timothy. He was taught about every conceivable subject in the ministry. Paul taught him about Bible study, about training of pastors and even about how to handle rebels. However, a good analysis of Paul's instructions to his son Timothy will reveal that the first command was to pray.

**I exhort therefore, that FIRST OF ALL supplications, prayers, intercessions, and giving of thanks, be made for all men. For kings and for all that are in authority; that we may lead a quiet and peaceable life in all godliness and honesty. For this is good and acceptable in the sight of God our Saviour.**

**1 Timothy 2:1-3**

This Scripture is usually referred to when the church is being taught about praying for the government. I agree that this verse is teaching us to pray for our leaders. But I want to draw your attention to the fact that it was the first major instruction that Paul gave to Timothy. And it was an instruction to pray. The first chapter of First Timothy does not contain any major commands to Timothy. In this all-important letter, the apostle found it important first of all to tell Timothy to pray.

A minister has many things to do, but *first of all* he must pray!

## 7. Pray because the Apostles refused to give up prayer when they were under pressure from administrative duties.

**Then the twelve called the multitude of the disciples unto them, and said, It is not reason that we should leave the word of God, and serve tables.**

**Wherefore, brethren, look ye out among you seven men of honest report, full of the Holy Ghost and wisdom, whom we may appoint over this business.**

**But we will give ourselves continually to prayer, and to the ministry of the word.**

**Acts 6:2-4**

When the early church grew the apostles came under pressure to become administrators.

The mystery of ministry is this - when you pray you will give birth to many souls and much fruit. These new fruits will demand care and time from you. Their needs will overwhelm you. You will have a genuine burden to help them. As you become engaged in helping these ones, you will find less time to pray. As you pray less, your ministry will plateau or decline. **Your greatest duty therefore, is to be able to balance the need to look after the souls and the need to pray.** I find myself struggling with this all the time.

Peter and the other apostles took the right decision and preserved their ministries. The baton has been handed over to us. Our greatest need is to spend hours in prayer. Let us not succumb to the pressure that wants us to neglect our great responsibility of intercession. If we neglect prayer, who will do it?

What is the difference between the living sections and the dead sections of the church today? It is prayer! The section that is alive is where the blood of Jesus is flowing and where people are being saved. Medically speaking, a person is alive when his heart beats and the blood flows through the body. A person is also declared to be alive when the doctor can hear air blowing through the lungs.

Spiritually speaking, when the blood of Jesus is flowing through the body and people are being saved, we can say that the church is alive. When the Holy Spirit is blowing through the body we can also say that the church is alive.

There are many churches where nobody is ever saved or filled with the Spirit. These are the dead parts of the church. There have always been dead parts of the church. Do you want your church to die? Do you want to be classified as a dead church? I hope not!

**I know thy works, that thou hast a name that thou livest, AND ART DEAD.**

**Revelation 3:1**

One of the hallmarks of what people call revival is prayer. Where do you hear shouting and prayer all night long? Where do you hear of long prayer meetings with people speaking in tongues? In such places you will see people being saved and filled with the Holy Spirit continually.

Do not take the subject of prayer lightly! Prayer is the lifeline to your ministry. That is why the apostles did not give up the ministry of prayer even when they were under pressure.

## 8. Pray because prayer was the greater part of Christ's ministry.

### 1 unit of preaching: 571.4 units of prayer

Think about it. Jesus preached and taught for three and a half years. Since then, He has been interceding for us. Three and a half years of teaching compared to two thousand years of prayer! This gives us a ratio of one unit of preaching for every five hundred and seventy one units of prayer That is an amazing ratio! **Most ministers have more than ten units of preaching to one unit of prayer!**

Perhaps you didn't know that Jesus is still carrying out His ministry towards us. The Bible teaches very clearly that Jesus is our shepherd and that He cares for us. Consider if you were a pastor caring for a congregation who had to travel abroad. Would your heart not be with the people you had left behind? Would you not pray for them? Would you not send messengers to them? Would you not send gifts to the congregation to help them along their way? This is exactly what is happening to Jesus. He keeps sending messages, gifts and blessings to us. Notice these revealing Scriptures.

**Wherefore he is able also to save them to the uttermost that come unto God by him, seeing HE EVER LIVETH TO MAKE INTERCESSION for them.**

**Hebrews 7:25**

**...it is Christ that died, yea rather, that is risen again, who is even at the right hand of God, WHO ALSO MAKETH INTERCESSION FOR US.**

**Romans 8:34**

Jesus is alive! He is able to save us to the uttermost. In other words, He is rescuing us from every extreme and distressing situation. We are being saved to the uttermost because of Jesus' prayer. Salvation is affecting every part of our lives because of Jesus' intercession. Think about how your converts would be saved to the uttermost if you prayed like Jesus prayed.

## Greatness in Ministry Depends on Intercessory Abilities

Even in the Old Testament, predictions were made about the great ministry of Jesus because He was going to be an intercessor. Intercession truly makes you into a great man of God. I have rarely seen a great man of God who is not a man of prayer. The cycle is like this: *man of prayer means man of faith means great man of God.*

**Therefore will I divide him A PORTION WITH THE GREAT, and he shall divide the spoil with the strong; he hath poured out his soul unto death: and he was numbered with the transgressors; and he bear the sin of many, and MADE INTERCESSION for the transgressors.**

**Isaiah 53:12**

Do you want to be numbered among the great and strong in God's army? Move away from debates, arguments and endless discussions. Become an intercessor today.

**9. Pray because prayer releases captives.**

If your eyes were opened spiritually you would suddenly see millions of people in spiritual captivity. They are captive to demon powers that are loose on this earth.

**...to preach deliverance to the captives.**

**Luke 4:18**

In my opinion, the people experiencing the strongest oppression are the people who live in Europe. Our duty as ministers is to *weaken* the grip of these demonic powers over the souls on this earth. At best our spiritual warfare can dislodge, displace or temporarily relocate demonic forces so that God's kingdom can gain ascendancy for a season.

**...pulling down of strongholds.**

**2 Corinthians 10:4**

The demons in the madman of Gadara wanted to stay in the area and they got their way in the end. Jesus only relocated them within the Gadara community. The Bible teaches that the devil has a right to be around. There is no use in trying to cast the devil out of the earth. Satan has a lease period that he is exploiting to the fullest. He reminded Jesus that he had a lease and a right to be around. He reminded Jesus that it was not yet time for them to be put out of the earth.

**...Jesus, thou Son of God art thou come hither to torment us BEFORE THE TIME?**

**Matthew 8:29**

A time will come when Satan will be permanently removed from the earth. We will not have to do that job. It will be done by a mighty angel from heaven. Our duty is just to weaken the stronghold so that some captives can escape. We can weaken the stronghold of the devil by prayer.

This is why the devil said: "have you come before the time?". The devil can also read and write and he sees his future judgement in black and white. When this happens he will no longer have the power to deceive and to destroy the people on this earth. Read it for yourself.

**And I saw an angel come down from heaven, having the key of the bottomless pit and a great chain in his hand. And he laid hold on the dragon, that old serpent, which is the Devil, and Satan, and bound him a thousand years. And cast him into the bottomless pit, and SHUT HIM UP, and set a seal upon him, that he**

**should DECEIVE THE NATIONS NO MORE, till the thousand years should be fulfilled: and after that he must be loosed a little season...**

**Revelation 20:1-3**

## One Thousand Years Later

**...And the devil that deceived them was cast into the lake of fire and brimstone, where the beast and the false prophet are, and shall be tormented day and night for ever and ever.**

**Revelation 20:10**

For now, the only thing we can do is to weaken the grip and hold of satanic power on the souls of men. When this grip is weakened, the captives will walk away in freedom. When you pray, the power of the devil to hold unbelievers is weakened. Our greatest weapon is prayer. That is why nothing happens when there is no prayer. That is why a lot happens when people pray! That is why the devil is doing everything to prevent you from praying.

**For the weapons of our warfare are not carnal, but mighty through God to the PULLING DOWN OF STRONGHOLDS.**

**2 Corinthians 10:4**

Because the devil knows that we have no weapons in the natural, he often tries to keep us operating in the natural realm. What a mistake it is to function mainly in the natural, a realm where we are unarmed and 'weaponless'! May the Lord open your eyes to understand this revelation of prayer!

10. **Pray because prayer availeth much.**

**Confess your faults one to another, and pray one for another, that ye may be healed. The effectual fervent prayer of a righteous man availeth much.**

**James 5:16**

The Bible teaches that prayer has great effects. Almost every Christian knows this famous scripture on the power of prayer.

21

The term "availeth much" is a little blind to us. Here are ten different definitions of this expression.

"To avail much" means:

a. *To succeed*
b. *To prevail*
c. *To overcome*
d. *To be able to do something*
e. *To be strong against an opposing force*
f. *To be helpful*
g. *To make an impact*
h. *To strike an impression*
i. *To be effective*
j. *To accomplish much.*

I also enjoy these translations of the Scripture - James 5:16

**Tremendous power is made available through a good man's earnest prayer.**
**James 5:16 (Philips Translation)**

**The prayer of a righteous man can bring powerful results.**
**James 5:16 (Olaf M Norlie Translation)**

**The prayer of a righteous man - makes tremendous power available - dynamic in its working.**
**James 5:16 (Amplified Translation)**

**An upright man's prayer, when it keeps at work is very powerful.**
**James 5:16 (Williams Translation)**

## Chapter 4

# Eighteen Facts about
# Spiritual Warfare

Spiritual warfare is the art of fighting against spiritual forces on the earth. These forces have captured the souls of millions. Like the Bible says, the devil has deceived the whole world. We may not be able to get rid of him now, but we will definitely weaken his grip on the masses through our prayer. We know that one day he will be dealt with permanently.

> **And I saw an angel come down from heaven, having the key of the bottomless pit and a great chain in his hand. And he laid hold on the dragon, that old serpent, which is the Devil, and Satan, and bound him a thousand years. And cast him into the bottomless pit, and SHUT HIM UP, and set a seal upon him, that he should DECEIVE THE NATIONS NO MORE, till the thousand years should be fulfilled: and after that he must be loosed a little season...**
>
> **Revelation 20:1-3**

> **...And the devil that deceived them was cast into the lake of fire and brimstone, where the beast and the false prophet are, and shall be tormented day and night for ever and ever.**
>
> **Revelation 20:10**

Let me now share with you twenty facts you should know about our battle with the demonic hordes on this earth.

### 1. Our principal enemy is Satan and not other human beings.

He is the leader of the hordes of demonic forces on this earth. Satan is a powerful being who fell from a glorious estate.

23

How art thou fallen from heaven, O Lucifer, son of the morning! How art thou cut down to the ground, which didst weaken the nations! For thou hast said in thine heart, I will ascend into heaven, I will exalt my throne above the stars of God: I will sit also upon the mount of the congregation, in the sides of the north: I will ascend above the heights of the clouds; I will be like the most High. Yet thou shalt be brought down to hell, to the sides of the pit.

They that see thee shall narrowly look upon thee, and consider thee, saying, Is this the man that made the earth to tremble, that did shake kingdoms; That made the world as a wilderness, and destroyed the cities thereof; that opened not the house of his prisoners? All the kings of the nations, even all of them, lie in glory, every one in his own house.

But thou art cast out of thy grave like an abominable branch, and as the raiment of those that are slain, thrust through with a sword, that go down to the stones of the pit; as a carcase trodden under feet.

Isaiah 14:12-19

2. **Satan, an intelligent being, has resorted to the warfare of deception, tricks and fantastic schemes.**

Satan, who is our principal enemy, knows that he does not stand a chance against the might of the church.

Put on the armour of God, that ye may be able to stand against the WILES of the devil.

Ephesians 6:11

3. **In order to defeat our enemy, we must know as much as we can about him.**

This is one of the most important rules of war. This is where secular armies engage in reconnaissance and intelligence work. Without this knowledge you will be defeated easily. Ask the US Army what happened to them in Vietnam.

## 4. Satan has a contagious nature/character which he passes on to his followers.

A lot of information about our enemy can be gleaned by analysing the twenty names and titles of Satan. Know your enemy so that you can defeat him.

## 5. Satan has a right to be on Earth.

He told Jesus that. He showed Jesus the nations of the world and offered them to Him. Jesus did not tell the devil that he was lying. He knew that the devil had the power to hand over the nations of the world. He did not argue about that. If it was not so, Jesus would not have been tempted.

> **And the devil said unto him, All this power will I give thee, and the glory of them: for that is delivered unto me; and to whomsoever I will I give it.**
>
> **Luke 4:6**

## 6. The Devil knows that he has a lease on the Earth.

This lease will expire soon and the devil knows it. Our enemy in spiritual warfare is the devil. Satan is aware of the expiry date on his lease.

> **And, behold, they cried out, saying, What have we to do with thee, Jesus, thou Son of God? art thou come hither to torment us BEFORE THE TIME?**
>
> **Matthew 8:29**

## 7. It is not our duty to rid the Earth of Satan and his demons.

Even Jesus did not try to do that! You do not try to get a tenant out of your house before the lease expires. You know that he will fight you in court. Our duty as ministers is to weaken the grip of demonic powers over the souls on this earth. At best our spiritual warfare can dislodge, displace or temporarily relocate demonic forces so that God's kingdom can gain ascendancy for a season.

...pulling down of strongholds.

**2 Corinthians 10:4**

**8.   Satan is a very wicked leasee.**

A lessee is a person who holds a property by lease.  Satan is the god of this world for a period.  The Bible tells us that the whole world lies in Satan's wicked arms because of this.

**And we know that we are of God, and THE WHOLE WORLD LIETH IN WICKEDNESS.**

**1 John 5:19**

The property that Satan the lessee has is trembling under his evil tenancy.  One day that power will be broken forever.

**9.   Even though we cannot get rid of the Devil permanently, we can engage him in different kinds of warfare.**

We can *wrestle* with him (Ephesians 6:12).  We can *cast* him out of people (Mark 5:13).  We can *bind* him (Matthew 18:18). We can *pull down* or weaken his strongholds (2 Corinthians 10:4).  We can *fight his deception* with the Word (Hebrews 4:12).

**10.   Satan's main strategy is to capture the world into groups of "strongholds" which think in a certain way.**

The devil's strategy is to make the world think in a certain way so that he can lead them into self-destruction.  The great philosophies of this world: humanism, atheism, communism and Marxism are manifestations of the imaginations of the devil.  It is these imaginations (trends of thinking) that lead masses of people into self-destruction.

**(For the weapons of our warfare are not carnal, but mighty through God to the pulling down of strong holds;)   CASTING DOWN IMAGINATIONS, and every high thing that exalteth itself against the knowledge of God, and bringing into captivity every thought to the obedience of Christ.**

**2 Corinthians 10:4,5**

## 11. Ministers must understand the role of the Word in spiritual warfare.

The church must destabilise and weaken strongholds on territories, nations, people and churches. All ministers must ensure that the Word of God gains pre-eminence. As the Word of God increases, Satan loses his grip over the souls. Read this amazing Scripture and believe in the power of the Word.

**And the WORD of God INCREASED; and the number of the DISCIPLES MULTIPLIED in Jerusalem greatly...**

**Acts 6:7**

**As the Word of God increases, the number of Christians will multiply.** That is why I write books and preach as hard as I can and as many times as possible. I know what it does to the kingdom of darkness.

## 12. Christian leaders must use the two-pronged weapon of prayer and the Word to defeat Satan in spiritual warfare.

The ministry of prayer and the ministry of the Word is real ministry. That is the two-edged weapon that God has given to us. The apostles practised this! They refused to be drawn away from the ministry of the Word and prayer.

**Then the twelve called the multitude of the disciples unto them, and said, It is not reason that we should leave the word of God, and serve tables. But we will give ourselves continually to PRAYER, and to the MINISTRY OF THE WORD.**

**Acts 6:2,4**

## 13. The best example of spiritual warfare was Christ Jesus.

He taught and He prayed.

**And in the morning, rising up a great while before day, he went out, and departed into a solitary place, and there prayed. And Simon and they that were with him**

27

followed after him. And when they had found him, they said unto him, All men seek for thee. And he said unto them, Let us go into the next towns, that I may preach there also: for therefore came I forth.

**Mark 1:35-38**

If we want to have the results that Jesus had, we must use the methods that He used. And His methods were praying and teaching.

## 14. Apart from weakening strongholds, ministers can dislodge, displace or temporarily relocate demonic forces so that God's kingdom can gain ascendancy.

In the ministry of Jesus, He relocated demons from people's bodies into swine.

And forthwith Jesus gave them leave. And the unclean spirits went out, and entered into the swine: and the herd ran violently down a steep place into the sea, (they were about two thousand;) and were choked in the sea.

**Mark 5:13**

## 15. Anytime you defeat (weaken or dislodge) the Devil, you can expect a counter attack.

When Jesus defeated the devil in the wilderness, the Bible says that Satan relocated for a season. The devil did not leave him forever. If you were the devil would you leave your enemy forever? No! You would retreat, regroup and attack again another day.

And when the devil had ended all the temptation, he departed from him FOR A SEASON.

**Luke 4:13**

## 16. Prayer and fasting are weapons that weaken and dislodge demonic forces.

Jesus taught that demons could be dislodged by prayer and fasting.

**Howbeit this kind GOETH NOT OUT BUT BY PRAYER and fasting.**

**Matthew 17:21**

## 17. The Word of God also weakens and torments Satan.

You will notice how the demon shouted out when Jesus taught the Word.

And there was in their synagogue a man with an unclean spirit; and he cried out, Saying, LET US ALONE; what have we to do with thee, thou Jesus of Nazareth?

Art thou come to destroy us? I know thee who thou art, the Holy One of God. And Jesus rebuked him, saying, Hold thy peace, and come out of him.

**Mark 1:23-25**

In this story, Jesus did not pray or bind the devil. But the devil said, "Stop it! You are tormenting me! You are hurting me!" The Bible describes the Word of God as a sword. Anytime you are speaking words, you are releasing swords into the atmosphere. Every pastor must use this great sword to achieve success in ministry.

## 18. Every minister must be careful of operating in the natural.

The Bible has warned us that we have no weapons in that realm.

**(For the weapons of our warfare ARE NOT CARNAL, but mighty through God to the pulling down of strong holds;)**

**2 Corinthians 10:4**

Because the devil knows that we are disarmed in the natural world he tries to keep us occupied in human, secular and natural things. That is why many ministers of the Gospel today are teachers, administrators, managers, etc. Be careful not to fall into this trap.

## Chapter 5

# Twenty Ways to Know Your Enemy so You Can Defeat Him

In order to defeat your enemy you must know as much as you can about him. This is one of the most common rules of war. This is why secular armies engage in reconnaissance and intelligence work. Reconnaissance is the art of discovering the strengths, weaknesses, plans and location of the enemy. Without this you cannot even start your war.

One of the ways by which we can know our enemy is to do a quick analysis of his names and titles. After all, a name speaks volumes about a person. Study the following twenty names or titles of Satan and you will know what you are dealing with.

## 1.   Devil

**Jesus answered them, Have not I chosen you twelve, and one of you is a DEVIL?**

**John 6:70**

The word 'devil' comes from the Greek word *diabolos*. This is where the English word diabolical comes from. *Diabolos* reveals the essential nature of this evil being. It means to be *inhumanly cruel* or *wicked*. It also means to be *outrageous* or *disgracefully bad*.

## 2.   Satan

**Now there was a day when the sons of God came to present themselves before the Lord, and SATAN came also among them.**

**Job 1:6**

This comes from a Hebrew word Satan, which literally means adversary. It speaks of being *diabolical* or *hellish*. This name was first used in the Book of Job. It described a very wicked being who murdered the entire household of Job and destroyed his business.

Satan is the archenemy of both God and man. In this interesting passage, Satan is spoken of as a real person who seemed to have access to heaven. He also seemed to have power to accuse the brethren and to seek their destruction.5

**3.   Accuser of the brethren**

**And I heard a loud voice saying in heaven, Now is come salvation, and strength, and the kingdom of our God, and the power of his Christ: for the ACCUSER OF OUR BRETHREN is cast down, which accused them before our God day and night.**

**Revelation 12:10**

This title explains the relentless accusations and slander that are hurled against God's servants.

**4.   Adversary**

**Be sober, be vigilant; because your ADVERSARY the devil, as a roaring lion, walketh about, seeking whom he may devour:**

**1 Peter 5:8**

This name reveals the antagonistic nature of Satan as he fights against everything we do.  No wonder there is such resistance, hostility and unfriendliness to the Gospel.

Satan's agents, the unbelievers, are often in tune with the spirit of opposition to the church and its leaders.  Many nations have laws that are hostile to the establishment of churches.  Even though churches have brought so much health and educational benefits to nations, political leaders have no choice but to oppose the church.

**5.   Angel of the bottomless pit**

**And they had a king over them, which is the ANGEL OF THE BOTTOMLESS PIT, whose name in the**

**Hebrew tongue is Abaddon, but in the Greek tongue hath his name Apollyon.**

**Revelation 9:11**

This name reveals the final destination of Satan and his cohorts. This can explain the frantic efforts of the devil to capture every corner of this earth. We must rise up now and counteract this desperate devil at every turn.

## 6. Belial

**And what concord hath Christ with BELIAL? Or what part hath he that believeth with an infidel?**

**2 Corinthians 6:15**

Belial means worthless. Satan is out to degrade you. Just observe someone who is under the influence of the devil. You will notice how worthless he becomes.

The devil degrades young men into becoming drug addicts, school dropouts, smugglers, etc. Belial turns young ladies into prostitutes with no sense of worth.

## 7. Beelzebub

**But when the Pharisees heard it, they said, This fellow doth not cast out devils, but by BEELZEBUB the prince of the devils.**

**Matthew 12:24**

This means the "Lord of the flies". A lord of flies is obviously a supervisor of disease and death. Satan is the author of the famine, disease and death that plague millions today.

## 8. God of this world

**In whom the GOD OF THIS WORLD hath blinded the minds of them which believe not, lest the light of the glorious gospel of Christ, who is the image of God, should shine unto them.**

**2 Corinthians 4:4**

"He's got the whole world in His hands." That's the song we

all learnt in Sunday school, but is that really the case? If He's got the whole world in His hands, then why are there so many wars and famines everywhere? Why is there such unhappiness in the world? Why is half of the world very rich and the other half very poor?

Certainly, this would not happen under the management and leadership of Jehovah. You see, Satan is actually the god of this world. Where Jehovah is in full control (heaven), the streets are made of gold and the people live in absolute bliss.

One day when the Lord takes over the rulership of this world, there will be a different kind of earth with love, peace, and joy.

## 9.   Murderer

**Ye are of your father the devil, and the lusts of your father ye will do. He was a MURDERER FROM THE BEGINNING, and abode not in the truth, because there is no truth in him. When he speaketh a lie, he speaketh of his own: for he is a liar, and the father of it.**
**John 8:44**

This is an appropriate title for the devil. He is a murderer. He is a killer and the author of all the bloodshed in this world. When he possesses a head of state this president may lead his nation into senseless wars which achieve nothing. As the fathers, husbands and brothers of multitudes are slaughtered, the murderer is living up to his reputation.

## 10.  Prince of devils

**But when the Pharisees heard it, they said, This fellow doth not cast out devils, but by Beelzebub the PRINCE OF THE DEVILS.**
**Matthew 12:24**

This title shows us the organised nature of the forces of darkness. Demons are organised into armies. They have an overall commander who is known as the prince of devils. As we move into spiritual warfare we are battling against an organized and intelligent enemy.

## 11. Prince of the power of the air

**Wherein in time past ye walked according to the course of this world, according to the PRINCE OF THE POWER OF THE AIR, the spirit that now worketh in the children of disobedience:**

**Ephesians 2:2**

This reveals Satan's control over the atmosphere and airwaves in any nation. Look closely at the radio and television waves of any nation. You will notice how Satan has dominated these fields. It is important for Christians to fight for the control of the airwaves. We must fight for the control of the arts, culture and the music of our nations. This is the domain of the prince of the power of the *air* and it is our duty is to dislodge him.

## 12. Prince of the world

**Hereafter I will not talk much with you: for the PRINCE OF THIS WORLD cometh, and hath nothing in me.**

**John 14:30**

This reveals Satan's rulership of the world and the systems of the world. As the world develops everything becomes more and more godless. I recently told a friend; "when I am in Europe I feel as though I am in Sodom." I said to him, "Europe is Pergamos revived!" Pergamos was the seat of Satan and the headquarters of demonic activity (Revelations 2:13).

## 13. The old serpent

**And THE SERPENT said unto the woman, Ye shall not surely die:**

**Genesis 3:4**

**And the great dragon was cast out, that OLD SERPENT, called the Devil, and Satan, which deceiveth the whole world: he was cast out into the earth, and his angels were cast out with him.**

**Revelation 12:9**

In the beginning, he was described as a serpent. In the end, he was described as a serpent. Snakes are some of the most dangerous creatures we know about. With one stroke, they can kill a human being. Yet, snakes manage to live near human beings without being detected. This is exactly how Satan works.

He is in the church and the people don't even know it. He is nearby causing damage and yet he is unseen.

As we battle against the devil, we must be constantly aware that even though he is invisible, he is real. Anytime I walk through tall grass I am conscious of the fact that there may be dangerous snakes nearby. Every pastor must be conscious of the fact that there may be invisible demonic activity nearby.

## 14. The tempter

**And when THE TEMPTER came to him, he said, If thou be the Son of God, command that these stones be made bread.**

**Matthew 4:3**

Satan is the author of temptation! He creates situations that test our resolve to obey God. He tempted Jesus and he will tempt you and I. But God will come to your rescue. He will provide a way of escape for every temptation.

## 15. Unclean spirit

**When the UNCLEAN SPIRIT is gone out of a man, he walketh through dry places, seeking rest, and findeth none.**

**Matthew 12:43**

The word unclean is used to describe the devil many times. This is because that is what the devil is. We are fighting a being that has a contagious nature that wants to make you unclean. The word unclean is translated from the Greek word *akarthartos*. It means impure, lewd, foul and unclean. It is a general term for Satan since his presence makes everything impure. Pure relationships are described as impure when unclean spirits get involved. Pure friendships become impure when the accuser points his finger at them.

## 16. The wicked one

**When any one heareth the word of the kingdom, and understandeth it not, then cometh the WICKED ONE, and catcheth away that which was sown in his heart. This is he which received seed by the way side.**

**Matthew 13:19**

The wickedness of the devil is unparalleled. Occasionally, human beings who have been greatly influenced by Satan display flashes of this hellish character. The wars of Sierra Leone, the genocide of Rwanda and Kosovo testify to the wickedness of Satan. This is the enemy we seek to dislodge and weaken. In the name of Jesus we will defeat the wicked one.

## 17. Lucifer

How art thou fallen from heaven, O LUCIFER, son of the morning! how art thou cut down to the ground, which didst weaken the nations! For thou hast said in thine heart, I will ascend into heaven, I will exalt my throne above the stars of God: I will sit also upon the mount of the congregation, in the sides of the north:

**I will ascend above the heights of the clouds; I will be like the most High. Yet thou shalt be brought down to hell, to the sides of the pit.**

**Isaiah 14:12-15**

Lucifer is the name given to the angelic being that fell from grace. Lucifer is described in great detail in the Book of Ezekiel.

**Thou hast been in Eden the garden of God; every precious stone was thy covering, the sardius, topaz, and the diamond, the beryl, the onyx, and the jasper, the sapphire, the emerald, and the carbuncle, and gold: the workmanship of thy tabrets and of thy pipes was prepared in thee in the day that thou wast created.**

**Thou art the anointed cherub that covereth; and I have set thee so: thou wast upon the holy mountain of God; thou hast walked up and down in the midst of the stones of fire. Thou wast perfect in thy ways from the day that thou wast created, till iniquity was found in thee.**

**Ezekiel 28:13-15**

You can see that he was an awesome being! The descriptions of his glory show us the kind of creature he is. If such a being is corrupted, you can understand the kind of monster that would be unleashed.

Satan's ability in the field of music (pipes and tabrets) is described in this passage. No wonder he has captivated millions through the power of unwholesome music.

## 18. Father of lies

**Ye are of your father the devil, and the lusts of your father ye will do. He was a murderer from the beginning, and abode not in the truth, because there is no truth in him. When he speaketh a lie, he speaketh of his own: for HE IS A LIAR, AND THE FATHER OF IT.**

**John 8:44**

When Saddam Hussein invaded Kuwait and declared war against the rest of the world, he frightened America by saying, "We're going to have the mother of all battles." When someone is described as a "mother" or "father", it tells us something important. If Satan is the father of lies then he is the parent and creator of all forms of deception. Satan's power to deceive is unparalled.

## 19. Abaddon

**And they had a king over them, which is the angel of the bottomless PIT, whose name in the Hebrew tongue is ABADDON, but in the Greek tongue hath his name Apollyon.**

**Revelation 9:11**

This is the angel of the abyss. In the Book of Job this word is translated destruction. *If you can't have it - destroy it!* This is the very nature of the devil. Some heads of state that cannot have power any longer, delight in destroying the entire nation through war. They get this idea from their master Abaddon.

## 20. Principalities, powers, rulers of darkness, wicked spirits

**For we wrestle not against flesh and blood, but against principalities, against powers, against the rulers of the darkness of this world, against spiritual wickedness in high places.**

**Ephesians 6:12**

In this Scripture, Paul groups the four main agents of Satan's outreach. Principalities represent spirits that dominate geographical areas. It is obvious that different kinds of spirits occupy different geographical areas. Amsterdam, for instance, has a principality of immorality. There is a saying that good boys go to heaven and bad boys go to Amsterdam.

Powers are beings that exert control over individuals. Another name you could give to them is "spirits that influence". Wicked spirits in high places speak of wicked entities that exist in the heavenlies. It was such a being that opposed the angel who was returning to Daniel with an answer to prayer (Daniel 10:13).

Rulers of the darkness speak of the spiritual beings that control the darkness in the world. The underworld and the unbelievers are all under influence without even knowing it.

## Chapter 6

# Five Ways for Pastors
# to Pray Effectively

**The EFFECTUAL fervent prayer of a righteous man availeth much.**

**James 5:16**

Not all prayers are effective prayers. **Some prayers are what I call doodling and dawdling prayers.** It is important to pray effectively in the ministry. You might as well be out there doing something less spiritual if your prayers are not going to work! You might as well say "twinkle, twinkle little star", if your prayers are not going to work.

I want to share with you five steps to praying effectively.

## 1.  Pray strategic Bible prayers.

Let your prayers be guided by the Word of God. Pray the prayers that are recorded in the Word of God. For instance Ephesians 1:17-19 contains one of the most powerful prayers a minister should pray. I have prayed this prayer for myself for many years. I suggest that you do the same. Another important prayer is found in Ephesians 3:15-19. This 'Bible strategic prayer' will make you pray to be grounded in love. This is very important for every pastor. Pastors make great sacrifices for the ministry but if they don't have love, they will lose their heavenly rewards. It is God's will that you reap the full benefits of your ministry in Heaven.

> **... though I give my body to be burned, and have not charity, it profiteth me nothing.**
> **1 Corinthians 13:3**

In a later chapter, I will share in more detail on why your prayers must be guided by the Word of God. Become a Word person. Trust yourself to God and His Word. Believe in the Word more than you believe in yourself.

## 2.  Pray fervently.

Praying fervently is one of the conditions for effective prayer. To pray fervently means to pray ardently, with passion and feeling. The word fervent means *passionate, enthusiastic, zealous, fanatical, impassioned, keen, avid, burning, ardent and eager.*

If someone is watching you pray, he should be able to describe your prayer with one of the words you just read. If that is how your prayer is, I assure you that you will have great results. Certainly, doodling and dawdling do not show fervency in prayer!

## 3.  Pray in tongues.

Every minister should spend several hours praying in tongues. Tongues is a gift that God has given to us. The Apostle Paul was very proud of his gift of tongues. He boasted: "I thank God that I speak in tongues more than you all." (1 Corinthians 14:18) By this gift we can speak to God in a supernatural way. The gifts of the Spirit are not intended to be unnecessary ornamental appendages that may or may not be used. **Use what God has given to you and you will be blessed in ministry.**

## 4.  Have discussions with the Holy Spirit.

Prayer should be a two-way affair. **If you want to develop in ministry you are going to have to learn to speak to the Holy Spirit.** You need to hear His voice as well. The Holy Spirit is to us what Jesus was to His disciples. Somebody to talk to when you need to. Ministers who engage in conversations with the Holy Spirit are often very advanced in their walk with God.

**I will not leave you comfortless: I will come to you. But the Comforter, which is the Holy Ghost, whom the Father will send in my name, he shall teach you all things, and bring all things to your remembrance, whatsoever I have said unto you.**

**John 14:18,26**

Take your prayer a step further. Speak to the Holy Spirit and hear Him speak back to you. You will have supernatural direction like you never imagined.

### 5.  Pray for a long time.

Two-minute prayers are different from hours of prayer. There is no scripture that says that if you do not pray for long hours God will not hear you. However, Jesus, the ultimate minister prayed for long hours. The example of Jesus is compelling enough to follow.

> **And in the morning, rising up A GREAT WHILE BEFORE DAY, he went out, and departed into a solitary place, and there prayed.**
>
> **Mark 1:35**

> **And it came to pass in those days, that he went out into a mountain to pray, and CONTINUED ALL NIGHT IN PRAYER to God.**
>
> **Luke 6:12**

As you can see, Jesus prayed for several hours. Paul was also someone who prayed for hours. Notice what he said in his letter.

> **NIGHT AND DAY PRAYING EXCEEDINGLY that we might see your face, and might perfect that which is lacking in your faith.**
>
> **1 Thessalonians 3:10**

## Chapter 7

# Six Reasons for Praying Strategic Bible Prayers

In this chapter I want to share how you can make your ministry of prayer effective. The lesson here is simple. Pray what I call Bible strategic prayers! What do I mean by Bible prayers? Bible prayers are prayer outlines that can be found in the Word of God. There are several prayer topics that are outlined in the Word.

### a.  The Lord's Prayer

After this manner therefore pray ye: Our Father which art in heaven, Hallowed be thy name. Thy kingdom come. Thy will be done in earth, as it is in heaven. Give us this day our daily bread. And forgive us our debts, as we forgive our debtors. And lead us not into temptation, but deliver us from evil: For thine is the kingdom, and the power, and the glory, for ever. Amen.

Matthew 6:9-13

### b.  First Ephesians prayer

Cease not to give thanks for you, making mention of you in my prayers; That the God of our Lord Jesus Christ, the Father of glory, may give unto you the spirit of wisdom and revelation in the knowledge of him: The eyes of your understanding being enlightened; that ye may know what is the hope of his calling, and what the riches of the glory of his inheritance in the saints, And what is the exceeding greatness of his power to us-ward who believe, according to the working of his mighty power.

Ephesians 1:16-19

### c.  Second Ephesians prayer

For this cause I bow my knees unto the Father of our Lord Jesus Christ, Of whom the whole family in heaven and earth is named, That he would grant you, according to the riches of his glory, to be strengthened with might by his Spirit in the inner man; That Christ may dwell in your hearts by faith; that ye, being rooted and grounded in love, May be able to comprehend with all saints what is the breadth, and length, and depth, and height; And to know the love of Christ, which passeth knowledge, that ye might be filled with all the fulness of God.

Ephesians 3:14-19

### d.   Timothy's prayer

I exhort therefore, that, first of all, supplications, prayers, intercessions, and giving of thanks, be made for all men; For kings, and for all that are in authority; that we may lead a quiet and peaceable life in all godliness and honesty. For this is good and acceptable in the sight of God our Saviour.

1 Timothy 2:1-3

I am not saying that these are the only things you should ever pray about. But I believe that if you make this your main prayer line you will see a change in your ministry. For further insight on this subject, see my book on Strategic Prayer.

I want to give you six reasons why you should stick to Bible prayers.

1.  **Human beings are corrupt in our minds, thoughts and in our hearts.** Very often our desires are corrupted by our corrupt human estate. No matter how spiritual a man of God is, he is at his best, still a man!

    For this corruptible must put on incorruption, and this mortal must put on immortality.

    1 Corinthians 15:53

2.  **We do not know what to pray for as we ought. No matter how spiritual we become we are unable to see things clearly.**

    ...for WE KNOW NOT what we should pray for as we ought...

    Romans 8:26

43

For now we see through a glass DARKLY…

1 Corinthians 13:12

This verse teaches us that we do not see things clearly. When you see a vision, what is actually happening is that you are *being drawn towards the spirit world.* The further out you are drawn, the clearer the vision becomes. In some cases, you are actually drawn out of your body. Like the apostle Paul said, he knew a man who was caught up to the third heavens.

I knew a man in Christ…such an one CAUGHT UP to the third heaven…How that HE WAS CAUGHT UP into paradise…

2 Corinthians 12:2,3,4

This man didn't even know whether he was in or out of his body. Most people are not drawn out very far and their visions are often a blurred picture that they are not certain of. In reality, a lot of what people call visions and prophecies are just impressions of things they see vaguely.

We need the help of the Holy Spirit to guide us, even in prayer. When we pray in tongues, the Holy Spirit controls our prayers. However, the Holy Spirit has already given us guidance for prayer through the words of Jesus and the letters of Paul. **If we follow these guidelines it will almost be equivalent to praying in tongues because the Word will guide us on what to pray for.**

3.  **Pray Bible strategic prayers because our ways are not His ways.**

For my thoughts are not your thoughts, neither are your ways my ways, saith the Lord.

Isaiah 55:8

No matter how spiritual we become we are still human beings in a container of flesh. I have found God teaching me things that I thought I knew. I would have raised the dead many years earlier in my ministry, but His ways were not my ways. I prayed and fasted that God would use me to raise the dead father of a good friend. But God didn't seem to take any notice of me. I felt let

44

down and disgraced. I had gone out there in faith, declaring that the dead would rise in the name of Jesus!

Unfortunately for me, my ways are not His ways. If that dead man had been raised, my entire life and ministry could have been ruined. God had His way and His way was to protect me and gently introduce me to real ministry.

Almost twenty years later, when a lady stood on my crusade platform testifying that her dead child had been raised as I ministered, I felt no emotion at all. I felt that if God wanted to raise the dead, it was entirely up to Him. I knew that I was an observer on the crusade platform. If this had happened twenty years earlier, perhaps I would have backslidden out of pride.

This is why we must pray more of Bible strategic prayers. God knows things that we do not know. Let us trust ourselves to His wisdom.

## 4. You must pray strategic Bible prayers to avoid missing the target.

The Bible teaches that many prayers miss the target. When your arrow misses the target, it means that it did not get where you intended it! Why should you pray without your prayers getting to the Father? Why should you pray without your prayers having the desired effect? It's time to stop missing the target.

Ye ask, and receive not, because YE ASK AMISS...

James 4:3

Why do so many prayers miss the target? Once again, it's because we are human. We cannot see clearly so we miss the target by miles. Trust yourself to Bible strategic prayers.

## 5. Bible strategic prayers cover all relevant areas that are important to your life.

If you go through the Lord's prayer, you will discover that every important area is covered. Under the Lord's strategic prayer, you pray for your daily needs, forgiveness, and protection for the work of God.

The Pauline prayers in the Book of Ephesians are a little more difficult to understand. The topics themselves seem to be mystical. Perhaps that is why they are even more important for us. You may never know the effect of praying for the Spirit of revelation and wisdom (Ephesians 1:17). For example, the second Ephesians prayer (Ephesians 3:17) teaches that we should be rooted and grounded in love.

Naturally speaking, it does not occur to most of us to pray that we will be established in Christian love. But when you understand that all good works that are performed outside Christian love amount to zero, perhaps you will understand why the Holy Spirit gave us that prayer. Notice this verse in 1 Corinthians 13:3.

And though I bestow all my goods to feed the poor, and though I give my body to be burned, and have not charity, it PROFITETH ME NOTHING.

1 Corinthians 13:3

It's a good thing for you to serve God, even paying the ultimate price for the ministry. However, in one stroke of a pen we are warned that without love all our good deeds will amount to zero.

## 6. Bible strategic prayers prevent you from leaving out vital areas of prayer.

When you pray these prayers you will cover all-important areas of your life. Perhaps you do not feel like praying for your government. There are some governments that one would naturally curse rather than pray for. However, if you follow the biblical pattern of prayer, you will pray for them rather than curse them.

I exhort therefore, that, first of all, supplications, prayers, intercessions, and giving of thanks, be made for all men; For kings, and for all that are in authority; that we may lead a quiet and peaceable life in all godliness and honesty.

1 Timothy 2:1,2

Deliver yourself from leaving out a vital area of prayer by following these biblical strategic prayers.

# Chapter 8

# Seven Examples of Praying Fervently

1. **Elijah's ardent prayer as he bent over asking for rain, remains the most well known example of fervent prayer.**

   And Elijah said unto Ahab, Get thee up, eat and drink; for there is a sound of abundance of rain. So Ahab went up to eat and to drink. And Elijah went up to the top of Carmel; and HE CAST HIMSELF DOWN UPON THE EARTH, AND PUT HIS FACE BETWEEN HIS KNEES. And said to his servant, Go up now, look toward the sea. And he went up, and looked, and said, There is nothing. And he said, Go again seven times.
   And it came to pass at the seventh time, that he said, Behold, there ariseth a little cloud out of the sea, like a man's hand. And he said, Go up, say unto Ahab, Prepare thy chariot, and get thee down, that the rain stop thee not. And it came to pass in the mean while, that the heaven was black with clouds and wind, and there was a great rain. And Ahab rode, and went to Jezreel. And the hand of the Lord was on Elijah; and he girded up his loins, and ran before Ahab to the entrance of Jezreel.

   1 Kings 18:41-46

   This is the classic example of fervent prayer that was spoken of by James. I see you praying fervently to release the rain of God's blessing on your ministry! Look at the example of Elijah as he prayed to God for rain.

2. **Hannah's tearful emotional prayer for a child also yielded fantastic results.**

   So Hannah rose up after they had eaten in Shiloh, and after they had drunk. Now Eli the priest sat upon a seat by a post of the temple of the LORD. And she was in bitterness of soul, and prayed unto the LORD, and wept sore.

And she vowed a vow, and said, O LORD of hosts, IF THOU WILT INDEED LOOK ON THE AFFLICTION OF THINE HANDMAID, AND REMEMBER ME, AND NOT FORGET THINE HANDMAID, BUT WILT GIVE UNTO THINE HANDMAID A MAN CHILD, THEN I WILL GIVE HIM UNTO THE LORD ALL THE DAYS OF HIS LIFE, AND THERE SHALL NO RAZOR COME UPON HIS HEAD. And it came to pass, as she continued praying before the LORD, that Eli marked her mouth.

Now Hannah, she spake in her heart; only her lips moved, but her voice was not heard: therefore Eli thought she had been drunken. And Eli said unto her, How long wilt thou be drunken? put away thy wine from thee. And Hannah answered and said, No, my lord, I am a woman of a sorrowful spirit: I have drunk neither wine nor strong drink, but have poured out my soul before the LORD. Count not thine handmaid for a daughter of Belial: for out of the abundance of my complaint and grief have I spoken hitherto.

Then Eli answered and said, Go in peace: and the God of Israel grant thee thy petition that thou hast asked of him. And she said, Let thine handmaid find grace in thy sight. So the woman went her way, and did eat, and her countenance was no more sad.

1 Samuel 1:9-20

Hannah was in serious trouble. She desperately needed a breakthrough. She didn't just doodle and dawdle. To doodle and dawdle means to hang around, loiter, waste time and to make wavy impressions. She was dead serious about what she wanted from God. Dear pastor, fervent prayer will make you give birth to a new dimension in ministry.

## 3. Jacob's all-night wrestling prayer yielded tremendous results.

And Jacob was left alone; and there WRESTLED A MAN with him until the breaking of the day.

Genesis 32:24

Jacob was blessed and so was his seed. Several thousand years have gone by but the fruit of this fervent prayer is evident for all to see. Israel still stands as one of the most favoured nations on the earth.

4.  **Moses' burning prayer for victory over Amalek, is another example of fervent prayer.**

    Then came Amalek, and fought with Israel in Rephidim. And Moses said unto Joshua, Choose us out men, and go out, fight with Amalek: to morrow I will stand on the top of the hill with the rod of God in mine hand. So Joshua did as Moses had said to him, and fought with Amalek: and Moses had said to him, and fought with Amalek: and Moses, Aaron, and Hur went up to the top of the hill. And it came to pass, when MOSES HELD UP HIS HAND, THAT ISRAEL PREVAILED: and when he let down his hand, Amalek prevailed. But Moses' hands were heavy; and they took a stone, and put it under him, and he sat thereon; and Aaron and Hur stayed up his hands, the one on the one side, and the other on the other side; and his hands were steady until the going down of the sun.

    Exodus 17:8-12

    When your children's lives are at stake you cannot afford to laze about. Doodling prayers never helped anyone!

5.  **David's passionate request that the Holy Spirit be not withdrawn from him was another example of a fervent prayer.**

    Have mercy upon me, O God, according to thy lovingkindness: according unto the multitude of thy tender mercies blot out my transgressions. Wash me thoroughly from mine iniquity, and cleanse me from my sin. For I acknowledge my transgressions: and my sin is ever before me. Against thee, thee only, have I sinned, and done this evil in thy sight: that thou mightest be justified when thou speakest, and be clear when thou judgest. Behold, I was shapen in iniquity; and in sin did my mother conceive me. Behold, thou desirest truth in the inward parts: and in the hidden part thou shalt make me to know wisdom. Purge me with hyssop, and I shall be clean: wash me, and I shall be whiter than snow. Make me to hear joy and gladness; that the bones which thou hast broken may rejoice. Hide thy face from my sins, and blot out all mine iniquities. Create in me a clean heart, O God; and renew a right spirit in me. CAST ME NOT AWAY FROM THY PRESENCE; AND TAKE NOT THY HOLY SPIRIT FROM ME.

Psalm 51:1-11

David knew what it meant if the Holy Spirit were to leave him. He couldn't afford to have that happen.

God does listen to passionate fervent prayers. He looks disdainfully at Christians who while away time just waiting for the prayer meeting to end.

## 6. The New Testament Church prayed fervently for the power of the Holy Spirit to be upon their leaders.

And being let go, they went to their own company, and reported all that the chief priests and elders had said unto them. And when they heard that, they lifted up their voice to God with one accord, and said, Lord, thou God, which hast made heaven, and earth, and the sea, and all that in them is: By stretching forth thine hand to heal; and that signs and wonders may be done by the name of thy holy child Jesus. And when they had prayed, the place was shaken where they were assembled together; and they were all filled with the Holy Ghost, and they spake the word of God with boldness.

Acts 4:23,24,30,31

God heard their prayer and look at the results. When a church begins to pray fervently there are always results. Sometimes, I look at people who claim to be having a prayer meeting. Some of them are sleeping and others are just whiling away the time. How would you feel if someone fell asleep whilst talking to you? You would think that he is either disrespectful or very uninterested in you.

7.  **Jesus prayed passionately for the will of God to be done in his life.**

Who in the days of his flesh, when he had offered up prayers and supplications with strong crying and tears unto him that was able to save him from death, and was heard in that he feared.

Hebrews 5:7

The evidence of this was when he began to sweat blood. Fervent prayer always works. The ministry of Jesus was a great success! You will have great success in your ministry when you learn how to pray fervently. Whenever you don't know what to do, do what Jesus did. Jesus shouted when he prayed! Jesus prayed until he was sweating! Read it for yourself!

And being in an agony he prayed more earnestly: and his sweat was as it were great drops of blood falling down to the ground.

Luke 22:44

# Chapter 9

# Seven Signs of Fervent Prayer

Since fervency in prayer is so important to achieve results, how can you know that you are praying fervently? I want to show you seven signs of fervent prayer. As usual, the best examples are in the Bible.

## 1.  The Posture

The ministry of Elijah has the most famous example of fervent prayer. It is interesting to note his posture when he prayed.

> **And Elijah went up to the top of Carmel; and he CAST HIMSELF DOWN upon the earth, and put his FACE BETWEEN HIS KNEES.**
> **1 Kings 18:42**

Begin to observe yourself and those around you at prayer meetings. What is their posture? Your posture speaks volumes about the kind of prayer you are engaged in.

## 2.  A Lifted Voice

When Jesus was on earth He prayed with loud cries and tears. Are your prayers soft or loud? Jesus prayed with strong cries and tears. I prefer to follow the example of Jesus!

> **Who in the days of his flesh, when he had offered up prayers and supplications with STRONG CRYING and TEARS unto him that was able to save him from death, and was heard in that he feared;**
> **Hebrews 5:7**

There are no meaningless details in the Bible. These things were written for our example. Let us learn from the heroes of faith.

## 3.  Weeping

Several Bible characters wept whilst they prayed. Our Lord

Jesus was the best example. Jesus offered up prayers with tears. There is nothing wrong with weeping whilst you pray. Jesus prayed fervent prayers and was heard by His Father.

Another famous prayer warrior was Hannah. Hannah was the mother of Samuel. The Bible describes her prayer time in graphic detail.

**And she was in bitterness of soul, and PRAYED UNTO THE LORD, AND WEPT SORE.**

**1 Samuel 1:10**

## 4. Exhaustion

Physical energy may be exacted from you when you pray. Jacob prayed all night. That must have been tiring. Jesus also prayed till everyone around Him fell asleep.

**And he cometh (after praying) and findeth his disciples asleep...**

**Matthew 26:40**

Moses prayed so hard that people had to help him lift up his hands.

**But Moses hands were heavy: and they took a stone and put it under him, and he sat thereon and Aaron and Hur stayed up his hands...**

**Exodus 17:12**

## 5. Quiet Groaning

**And it came to pass, that she continued praying before the Lord, that Eli marked her mouth. Now Hannah, SHE SPAKE IN HER HEART; ONLY HER LIPS MOVED.**

**1 Samuel 1:12**

This was definitely an example of fervent prayer. This woman prayed passionately for a child. There was no shouting or screaming. The Bible says that Eli could not hear what she was praying about. He even thought she was drunk. This is what I call quiet groaning.

Jesus was another example of someone who groaned in prayer.

**When Jesus therefore saw her weeping, and the Jews also weeping which came with her, HE GROANED IN THE SPIRIT, and was troubled.**

**John 11:33**

## 6.    Inner Determination

Determination is not easily manifested. It is a quiet resolve to pray until something happens.  Anyone who is determined to pray until something happens is a passionate or fervent prayer warrior.

**And he said, Let me go, for the day breaketh.  And he said, I WILL NOT LET THEE GO, EXCEPT THOU BLESS ME.**

**Genesis 32:26**

People who come for prayer meetings without a determination to receive something from God often doodle and dawdle until the meeting is over.  Be determined to get answers for all your prayer requests!

## 7.    Desperate Language

If you study the prayers of David as recorded in the Psalms you will find the language of a desperate man.  David was a man who was looking for God's help.  A man reaching out frantically for the hand of God. Remember this: *God listens to every word you say.*  The words you speak matter!  Look at one example of King David's prayers.

**In thee O Lord, do I put my trust; LET ME NEVER BE ASHAMED: deliver me in thy righteousness.  Bow down thine ear to me; DELIVER ME SPEEDILY: be thou my strong rock, for AN HOUSE OF DEFENCE TO SAVE ME.  For thou art my rock and my fortress; therefore for thy name sake lead me, and guide me.**

**Psalm 31:1-3**

## Chapter 10

# Nine Steps to Praying for a Long Time

**1. Accept the fact that prayer that is less than one hour is not significant prayer for a minister.**

**Could you not watch with me for ONE HOUR?**

**Matthew 26:40**

For as long as I can remember, I have always considered short prayer insignificant. I have always felt that unless I spent a long time in prayer, I would not accomplish much. This has been a good psychological guide for me. It has made me spend many hours of my life in prayer.

When you believe that prayer for less than an hour is not enough, you will never be satisfied with five and ten minute prayers. This will gradually propel you into lengthy periods of prayer. You will not lose anything by praying for long periods of time!

**2. Always pray with a clock or a watch in view.**

As soon as you begin to pray, look at the time. When you do that, you will be compelled to spend a decent period of time in prayer. When you do not look at your watch you will think that you prayed longer than you actually did. You will tell yourself, "Oh, I must have prayed for two hours" when you only prayed for ten minutes.

Unless you are experienced in prayer, you will make wrong judgements about the length of time you have prayed. Nowadays, I can tell when I have prayed for an hour. Initially, I would pray for ten minutes and think it was an hour. This is why you need to keep an eye on the clock.

## 3. Pray with preaching tapes.

I always pray with some kind of preaching or music in the background. There is a principle I want you to understand. **The speed of preaching/music is a hundred times faster than the speed of silence.** This means that time runs a hundred times faster when there is some kind of background preaching or music.

Have you ever been there when people were asked to observe a minute's silence? Have you noticed how long the period of silence was? Did you know that they never really spend a *whole minute* of silence? This is because of the principle I just shared with you: *the speed of preaching/music is a hundred times faster than the speed of silence.* When you pray with the sound of preaching or music in the background, time runs much faster! Before you know it, you would have accomplished several hours in prayer!

The sound of the preaching of the Word of God creates a very conducive atmosphere for spiritual things. Dear friend, we are constantly bombarded with the secular environment of our jobs, of godless friends and of television. This kind of atmosphere actually prevents prayer. The environment in our homes is often anti-prayer. You need something that will keep you in a prayer mood for at least one hour. Sometimes the message on the tape will spur you on to continue in the Spirit! Try it and you will never be the same again.

## 4. Pray with music in the background.

**...now bring me a minstrel. And it came to pass, when the minstrel played, that THE HAND OF THE LORD CAME upon him.**

**2 Kings 3:15**

Godly music creates a beautiful worship environment. The Bible calls it the hand of the Lord. I always play music or preaching tapes when I am praying. Dear friend, the very atmosphere of our world is charged with demonic entities. The prince of the power of the air and his cohorts pollute the very air we breathe. It is difficult to pray in such an environment. This is the reason why many Christians do not pray for long hours. They are operating in a difficult atmosphere.

**But there is good news: You can have your own little church service wherever you are!** The Spirit of the Lord can move over you in your car. This has happened to me many times. I consider my car as a prayer closet. Invest whatever it takes to create the right prayer atmosphere.

The Spirit of the Lord will come upon you as you stay in the environment of anointed minstrels.

## 5. Pray with a preaching video.

Sometimes, the sound of preaching or the sound of music is not enough to get you into the right flow for prayer. At times, you need to have the video dimension. Sometimes both seeing and hearing are needed to create the right atmosphere for successful prayer. I often pray with a preaching video. I receive great blessings when I operate in the right environment.

## 6. Pray 90% of your prayer in tongues.

Tongues are a gift from God. This gift helps you to pray whilst your mind is inactive.

**For if I pray in an unknown tongue, my spirit prayeth, but my understanding is unfruitful.**
**1 Corinthians 14:14**

As you pray in tongues for hours, your spirit man will be edified and charged up.

## 7. Read the Bible and other Christian books as you pray.

Because I pray in tongues for long periods, my mind is free for reading. I constantly read whilst I spend hours in prayer. My spirit prays to the Lord while my mind concentrates on the Bible that I am reading. This helps me to pray even longer hours.

## 8. Disconnect your phone.

**The telephone is a favourite tool that is used by the devil to**

**interrupt your prayer.** With the feeling that you might receive an important call lingering in your mind, you are unable to switch off your phone. Most of us are unable to switch off our phones.

Needless interruptions break up our precious hour of prayer into thirty minutes of piecemeal five-minute sessions. I don't know if it happens to you. But as soon as I am getting into deep fellowship with the Lord, the phone rings! Sometimes it is so painful to receive an unnecessary call at the wrong time.

I have decided that if I am serious about praying I must disconnect my phone. The world can wait. Everything can wait until I finish talking to my Lord. When I do not disconnect my phone, it means only one thing: I am not serious about the prayer time!

**9. Issue a 'do not disturb' notice.**

Since you do not live on an island, you are going to need the co-operation of the people who live with you. If you are going to have an effective prayer life, people must know when you are praying. Just as they wouldn't disturb you if you were in the bathroom, they must not disturb you when you are in prayer! Do not be ashamed to let your friends and people at home know that you are in prayer and should not be disturbed.

Whilst in school, I was particularly impressed with a friend's ability to issue strong "do not disturb" notices. I always remember the notice he put outside his box room to ward off other students. It read something like this,

## Notice

*If you knock on this door*
*and receive no response from within*
*do not continue knocking or call for me.*
*If you do anything which contradicts this simple instruction*
*be it known unto you*
*that this door will not be opened unto you*
*no matter who you are!!!*

Such notices are very good! I once had to warn the workers in my house. I told them that if they called me whilst I was in prayer, I would dismiss them immediately. This gave me great freedom for prayer in my own home.

## Chapter 11

# Two Steps to Understanding Intercession

The word intercede comes from the Latin word *'intercedere'*. This word means to **intervene, interfere or to mediate.**

**And he saw that there was no man, and wondered that there was no intercessor: therefore his arm brought salvation unto him; and his righteousness, it sustained him.**

**Isaiah 59:16**

God has called every minister to *interfere* with Satan's plans to destroy the church. We have to rise up and *intervene* as the hordes of demons destroy young Christians. We must *interfere* with every demonic agenda to destroy the kingdom of God.

1. **To intercede means to come between so as to modify the course of events.**

Satan's plan is to lead entire nations to hell. By the power of intercession, we will modify the course of history. People who should have gone to hell will be saved. **Powerful men of intercession are constantly modifying the course of events.**

2. **To intercede means to be situated between things.**

God has called every minister to be situated between the devil and God's people. **That is what a shepherd does. He is situated between the wolves and the sheep.** The wolves and jackals do not have access to the sheep because of the shepherd's presence.

**And I sought for a man among them, that should make up the hedge, and stand in the gap before me for the land, that I should not destroy it: but I found none.**

**Ezekiel 22:30**

Intercession means to stand in the gap. It means to become an obstacle to Satan and his agents. Dear man of God, you are doing a good work. Dear missionary, your presence in that nation stands as a veritable rock of protection for many souls. Do not give up! Keep up the good work! Pray for the people God has given to you! *You are the last barrier between those precious souls and the enemy.*

## Chapter 12

# Twenty Reasons Why Every Pastor Needs an Intercessor

When you understand what intercession does, you will never stop praying for ministers. Our existence on this earth is constantly under threat. Although we don't realise it, we are in danger from so many things. Intercession comes in as a blockade between you and those perils. Sometimes we are so vulnerable and we don't even know it!

Remember that *to intercede means to intervene, interfere or to mediate.* Intercession means to come between so as *to modify the course of events.* An interceding person becomes *situated between things.*

When Paul listed the dangers he had been through as a minister, he was actually making a list of things that he needed intercession for.

Are they ministers of Christ? (I speak as a fool) I am more; in LABOURS more abundant, in STRIPES above measure, in PRISONS more frequent, in DEATHS oft.

Of the Jews five times received I FORTY STRIPES save one. Thrice was I BEATEN with rods, once was I STONED, thrice I suffered SHIPWRECK, a night and a day I have been in THE DEEP;

In JOURNEYINGS often, in perils of WATERS, in perils of ROBBERS, in perils by mine own COUNTRYMEN, in perils by the HEATHEN, in perils in the CITY, in perils in the WILDERNESS, in perils in the SEA, in perils among FALSE BRETHREN;

In WEARINESS and PAINFULNESS, in watchings often, in HUNGER and THIRST, in fastings often, in COLD and NAKEDNESS. Beside those things that are without, that which cometh upon me daily, the care of all the churches.

Who is weak, and I am not weak? who is offended, and I burn not?

2 Corinthians 11:23-27,29

The twenty dangers that the apostle Paul encountered are actually the twenty reasons why every minister needs prayer.

# Twenty Dangers That an Apostle Encounters

1. Labours more abundant (long hours of work)

2. Stripes above measure (unbearable physical afflictions)

3. Prisons more frequent (political and governmental harassment)

4. Deaths oft (near death experiences)

5. Forty stripes save one (special personalised intimidation)

6. Beaten with rods (having rubbish thrown at you)

7. Once stoned (mob attacks, breaking of walls and political hatred)

8. Shipwrecked three times (the danger of car, train and plane crashes)

9. The deep (the danger of drowning)

10. Journeyings often (the danger of travelling and accidents)

11. Perils of waters (the danger of eating and drinking things you're not used to)

12. Perils of robbers (theft of church properties, offerings, mobile phones)

13. Perils in the city (prostitution, immorality, muggings, armed robbers)

14. Perils in the wilderness (the danger of being a foreigner)

15. Perils of the sea (more dangers for the travelling minister)

16. Perils among false brethren (spies in the church, secret service agents everywhere, disloyal people)

17. In hunger (no money for food)

18. In thirst (no money for drinks)

19. In cold (danger of inadequate heating, risk of catching infections)

20. In nakedness (no appropriate clothes, winter coats, etc.).

## Chapter 13

# How to Intercede against the Law of Degeneration

M an's need for an intercessor is not always apparent. Throughout the Bible there have always been men who stood in the gap for other men. We often think that intercession just prevents *the devil* from attacking Christians. Intercession deals with much more than that. It deals with certain laws that are in place in the earth today. When you understand these things, you will always want to pray for your church members.

Remember again the definitions of intercession: to intercede means *to intervene, interfere or to mediate.* Intercession means to come between so as *to modify the course of events.* An interceding person becomes *situated between things.*

## Intercession Deals with the Law of Decay in the Church

**Yet I have planted thee a noble vine, holy a right seed: how then ART THOU TURNED INTO THE DEGENERATE PLANT of a strange vine unto me?**
**Jeremiah 2:21**

Whether we like it or not, there is a law of degeneration at work in the earth. Everything we create begins to decay the day after it is completed. Every building decays as the years go by. Our bodies gradually degenerate as the years go by. Just look at your picture ten years ago and you will understand what I am talking about. Wealth does not remain in one place forever. You may be rich today but your wealth may decay into nothing after ten years. There are cities that were very wealthy years ago. Today, these places have degenerated into large slums.

*To degenerate means to gradually become of a lower type. It is a gradual falling off to a lower form of development.*

The church is no different.  We are all under this law of degeneration.  This is why shepherds are advised to look to the state of their flocks.  If you leave a vibrant fellowship of Christians for three years without investing into it, it will decay.  And that without remedy!  You have to invest into it spiritually.

**Be thou diligent to know the state of thy flocks, and look well to thy herds.  For RICHES ARE NOT FOREVER; and doth the crown endure to every generation?**
**Proverbs 27:23,24**

The degeneration of a church can be defined as: *"to sink below a former or normal condition or character"*.  Degeneration also means *to deteriorate from a former standard.*  This law of degeneration is at work in your church, and in your members.  It affects all of us.  This is why you need to intercede for your people.  The law of degeneration is making the zealous ones less zealous.  The law of degeneration is working on the sweet prayerful Christians.  It is making them lose interest in prayer.  The law of degeneration is working against the holy Christians.  It is making them to deteriorate into immoral backsliders.  Dear pastor, you cannot sleep anymore.  The law of degeneration is at work in your church.  You need to rise up and intercede!

Have you noticed how people start their Christian lives with such a zeal for witnessing and preaching the Word?  Not long after, you hardly find them in church.  What has happened?  The law of degeneration!

This is why it is so important to keep intercession and prayer alive in the church!

*Chapter 14*

# How to Intercede against the Law of the World

## Intercession Deals with the Law of the World

**Love not the WORLD, neither the things that are in the world. If any man love the world, the love of the Father is not in him. For all that is in the WORLD, the lust of the flesh, and the lust of the eyes, and the pride of life, is not of the Father, but is of the world. And the WORLD passeth away, and the lust thereof: but he that doeth the will of God abideth forever.**

**1 John 2:15-17**

The world has a pervasive influence on the Church. Much of the church has become worldly and secular. This happens because the Church is "plum in the middle" of the world.

Intercession needs to go on so that the church does not become worldly. The things that are in the world, the lusts of the flesh and the lust of the eyes, stick themselves on to ministers without our even knowing it.

Man needs an intercessor! Demas needed an intercessor. He fell in love with the world and backslid. Fewer of our church members will backslide when we intercede for them. Intercession deals with the law of the world.

**For Demas hath forsaken me, having loved this present world...**

**2 Timothy 4:10**

*Chapter 15*

# How to Intercede against the Law of the Flesh

## Intercession Deals with the Law of the Flesh

Man has a need for an intercessor! The law of the flesh works against everything spiritual. Paul was afraid of his own flesh. He said he knew that there was nothing good in his flesh.

**For I know that in me (that is, in my flesh) dwelleth no good thing: for to will is present with me; but how to perform that which is good I find not.**

**Romans 7:18**

At one point, Paul said that he had lost confidence in his flesh.

**For we are the circumcision, which worship God in the spirit, and rejoice in Christ Jesus, and have no confidence in the flesh.**

**Philippians 3:3**

Dear friend, if Paul had lost confidence in his flesh, what should we do? The flesh is ready to take you to hell. The flesh is working against church growth. The flesh is working against the very life of the church. Your flesh is working against your spiritual progress.

The flesh makes the church members desire the wrong things and do the wrong things. It is the flesh that makes church members lazy. It is because of the flesh that most church members do not come to church every Sunday. When a pastor thinks of his children in the Lord, his heart must burn with interventionary prayer. *Father, help your children! Don't let them fall by the wayside.*

**But I keep under my body, and bring it into subjection: lest that by any means, when I have preached to others, I myself should be a castaway.**

**1 Corinthians 9:27**

Another need for intercession is in the area of sickness and disease. Intercessory prayer prevents disease from fastening its hold on people. Remember that it is easier to prevent diseases than to treat them. Intercessory prayer will prevent the pastors from conducting unnecessary funerals.

## Chapter 16

# How to Intercede against the Law of the Elements

## Intercession Deals with the Law of the Elements

What are the elements? The elements are the earth, the wind, the fire and the water. Whether you know it or not, these elements can turn against your existence. We need intercession so that these elements are kept at bay. When the elements turn against you, your ministry could be over. This is what happens when there are earthquakes, fires, floods and storms.

During Jesus' ministry on earth, He had to deal with the elements. The elements were trying to end His life and ministry.

**And when he was entered into a ship, his disciples followed him. And, behold, there arose a great tempest in the sea, insomuch that the ship was covered with the waves: but he was asleep. And his disciples came to him, and awoke him, saying, Lord, save us: we perish. And he saith unto them, Why are ye fearful, O ye of little faith? Then he arose, and rebuked the winds and the sea: and there was a great calm. But the men marvelled, saying, What manner of man is this, that even the winds and the sea obey him!**

**Matthew 8:23-27**

The disciples were amazed at how the elements responded to prayer commands. As you intercede for your people, they will be protected from any antagonistic elements in the earth. Sometimes it's the elements that bring about plane crashes, car pileups and other disasters. I see you rising up with the spirit of intercession for your people! Your ministry will be transformed.

*Chapter 17*

# How to Intercede against
# the Law of Humanity

## Intercession Deals with the Law of Humanity

The law of humanity deals with human nature. Here, we deal with two main areas:

a.  The reality of human nature.

b.  The reality of human error.

The human nature of ingratitude, forgetfulness and wickedness is well known. You do not have to look far to see a real war taking place. The wickedness in human nature is there for everyone to see. The genocide and brutal killings are evident.

Jesus was aware of how human beings could turn against Him.

**But Jesus did not commit himself unto them, because he knew all men, And needed not that any should testify of man: for he knew what was in man.**
**John 2:24,25**

When the tide of human nature turned against Christ, His miracles did not mean much anymore. They murdered Him within forty-eight hours. Do not underestimate the evil that is in man.

Our intercessory prayer works against the tide of human ungratefulness and forgetfulness in ministry. Dear pastor, when you pray for your congregation, it will help them not to forget the love you have bestowed on them.

Human error is often the cause for human disasters like the Titanic sinking or the Paddington train crash in London or the Concorde disaster.

Intercessory prayer will intervene to prevent human error from eliminating you.

As a doctor, I have seen other doctors make mistakes. I have watched people die as a result of human error. I once watched a consultant gynaecologist perform a major operation (laparotomy) on a young eleven-year-old girl. He thought she had a tumour in the lower abdomen. When they opened her up, all she had was compact faeces in the colon. This poor girl had been subjected to a major operation because the doctor did not examine her properly. All that this poor little girl needed was some medicine to make her go to the toilet! Other patients have died because surgeons forgot to remove some swabs or scissors from the abdomen before closing up.

Even when medicine is being practised, intercessory prayer is needed for protection against human error. This is why we pray for people when they are receiving any kind of medical treatment.

I watched a documentary called Flights from Hell. On this documentary, a pilot discovered that one of the wheels on the undercarriage was not coming out. This was because somebody (human error) had forgotten to remove the chock from the undercarriage. I watched the plane undergoing amazing manoeuvres to get the wheel out. In the end, the plane was forced to land on one wheel. It was a very lucky escape for everyone on the flight.

On another of these Flights from Hell, there was a flight from Bogota, Columbia to New York City. When the pilot got to New York, he was asked to go into a holding position and wait for his turn to land. He was kept in the air for over an hour.

The tragic thing about this story was that the pilot failed to communicate to the air traffic control tower that he was running out of fuel and how he urgently needed to land.

Can you believe that the pilot circled with this plane until *every drop* of fuel was finished and then crashed just outside the airport? Who ever heard of a jetliner crashing because it ran out of fuel? It was later established that the pilot failed to communicate the urgency of his situation (human error) to the control tower. I tell you, the people in that plane needed intercessory prayer very badly. The passengers were in the hands of a very dangerous man.

Intercessory prayer will intervene to protect your people from human *error* and human *nature*.

## Chapter 18

# How to Intercede against the Law of Nature

## Intercession Deals with the Law of Nature

When nature works against you, you will find yourself sweating! Nature speaks of the cycles and the seasons of the earth. It is about the natural things that God has created. When natural cycles change their usual character there are all sorts of problems. For instance, there are droughts, famines, floods and tornadoes. What is happening is the distortion of natural things. When a natural wave of the ocean becomes enlarged then you have a tidal wave.

When you fall into the sea and the tide takes you away, you are in the hands of nature. **Wild animals, insects, viruses, bacteria and parasites are all manifestations of nature turning against man.**

I was once on a safari in South Africa. There were all sorts of wild animals in the park. I asked our guide if it was safe to get out and walk.

He said to me, "I wouldn't do that!"

You see, if I had walked alone in that safari park, I would have been at the mercy of nature. I would have subjected myself to the dangerous elements of nature.

The psalmist teaches about how blessed it is to have nature working in your favour. He predicts that anyone who walks in the Word of the Lord will have the seasons and the cycles working normally for him. When a woman is unable to have a child, a very natural process has been interrupted.

**Blessed is the man that walketh not in the counsel of the ungodly, nor standeth in the way of sinners, nor**

**sitteth in the seat of the scornful. But his delight is in the law of the LORD; and in his law doth he meditate day and night. And he shall be like a tree planted by the rivers of water, that bringeth forth his fruit in his season; his leaf also shall not wither; and whatsoever he doeth shall prosper.**

**Psalm 1:1-3**

Bacteria and viral infections are a further distortion of nature. Bacteria, if you like, are like microscopic wild animals that can kill you. When they cross your path, nature has begun to work against you.

Intercession is needed to prevent the forces of nature from consuming you. Intercessory prayer can even stop what people may call "natural deaths". Intercessory prayer leads people into the Word, so that they can have the blessings of Psalm 1.

When a person is ungodly, he falls into the hands of nature, and nature blows him away. Read it for yourself!

**The ungodly are not so: but are like the chaff which THE WIND DRIVETH AWAY.**

**Psalm 1:4**

## Chapter 19

# How to Intercede against
# the Law of the Devil

## Intercession Deals with the Law of the Devil

The law of the devil teaches that there is a devil out there. This devil and his agents are actively working against our lives. I have seen the devil twice! On both occasions he was trying to destroy me. Suddenly my eyes were open and I was able to see my enemy clearly. This is what happened to Paul in Macedonia.

He was harassed by a demon for several days. Suddenly the Lord gave him a manifestation of the gift of discerning of spirits. This allowed him to know exactly what he was dealing with. He cast out the devil and that was the end of the harassment.

**And it came to pass, as we went to prayer, a certain damsel possessed with a spirit of divination met us, which brought her masters much gain by soothsaying: The same followed Paul and us, and cried, saying, These men are the servants of the most high God, which show unto us the way of salvation. And this did she many days. But Paul, being grieved, turned and said to the spirit, I command thee in the name of Jesus Christ to come out of her. And he came out the same hour.**

**Acts 16:16-18**

### I Saw the Devil

On both occasions when I had a manifestation of discerning of spirits, the devil was at my right hand side. On one occasion, I saw the devil as a little monkey sitting on my bedside table. I was so surprised to see the devil so close! Suddenly, I was able to deal with this thing that was trying to eliminate me. If I had not dealt with that demon I may not be alive today.

# I Saw the Devil Again

On another occasion, my eyes were open to the spirit realm and I saw an eight-foot tall, blackened sooty figure suspended on the right side of my bed. I was startled and jumped out of bed and began to pray. The Lord had suddenly shown me the source of a severe and prolonged attack I had been experiencing in my ministry. I rose out of bed and the rest is history.

On both these occasions, the devil came very close to eliminating me. This is what is happening to pastors. This is why pastors need intercessors to pray for them.

This is what is happening to your church members. The enemy is after their souls. Intercede for them! Intervene in the situation! Get in the way and stand between the devil and the sheep that God has given to you! Transform your ministry by intercessory prayer.

## Chapter 20

# How to Intercede against the Law of Time

## Intercession Deals with the Law of "Time"

To every thing there is a season, and a time to every purpose under the heaven: A time to be born, and a time to die; a time to plant, and a time to pluck up that which is planted; A time to kill, and a time to heal; a time to break down, and a time to build up; A time to weep, and a time to laugh; a time to mourn, and a time to dance; A time to cast away stones, and a time to gather stones together; a time to embrace, and a time to refrain from embracing; A time to get, and a time to lose; a time to keep, and a time to cast away; A time to rend, and a time to sew; a time to keep silence, and a time to speak; A time to love, and a time to hate; a time of war, and a time of peace.

Ecclesiastes 3:1-8

The law of time teaches us that there is a time for everything. In your life, there will be a time to sow and a time to reap. There will be times of rejoicing and there will also be times of sorrow. There will be times when you will be up and other times when you will be down!

As the events of time unfold in your life, will you survive each season? When the time for prosperity comes, will you backslide or will you remain in the Lord? The children of Israel were warned of a time of prosperity. Moses warned them not to forget their God at that time. People simply need intercession because they enter into a new time or period of their lives.

Many people fall away in the day of their prosperity. Pastors need to pray for their congregations so that the little children (sheep) will not fall away in their time of temptation.

The Bible speaks of an evil day. An evil day is a day when things are not good. Intercession for believers will help them to stand in an evil day.

**Wherefore take unto you the whole armour of God, that ye may be able to withstand in the evil day, and having done all, to stand.**

**Ephesians 6:13**

If you are not praying for your people, when they enter into an evil day, they will fall! It is the duty of pastors and shepherds to constantly intercede for the sheep. **Every sheep is in a different time of his life.** God is expecting you to pray for your people because every one of them is in a different season of his existence.

Some people are in the season of temptation and death. They don't stand a chance unless you intercede for them!

## Chapter 21

# How to Intercede against the Law of Creeping Things

## Intercession Deals with the Law of Creeping Things

And God made the beast of the earth after his kind, and cattle after their kind, and everything that creepeth upon the earth after his kind: and God saw that it was good. And God said, Let us make man in our image, after our likeness: and let them have dominion over the fish of the sea, and over the fowl of the air, and over the cattle, and over all the earth, and over every creeping thing that creepeth upon the earth.

Genesis 1:25,26

What are creeping things? Creeping things are things that sneak up on you without you realising. The Book of Genesis speaks of the different creatures created by God. One group of creatures was called creeping things.

Spiritually speaking, there are things that move upon us stealthily. Great changes take place over a long period of time. Most people hardly notice when these changes are taking place.

Let me give your four things that creep upon all churches:

a.  Deception (e.g., the churches of Europe)

b.  Wrong attitudes (e.g., laziness, complacency and unbelief)

c.  Familiarity (e.g., not appreciating the gift of God in your midst)

d.  Shifting of priorities (e.g., becoming health and educational organisations instead of being missionary societies)

## Deception Is a Creeping Thing

How do you think the church in Europe degenerated from being a vibrant, missionary-minded society to becoming an atheistic and godless organisation? It did not happen over night. The spirit of deception crept on the church slowly. Deception is a creeping thing.

Familiarity is one of the most dangerous creeping things that invade the church. Without even realising it, the church does not hold their pastor in esteem. Of course, they claim they do, but in reality they do not!

## Familiarity Is a Creeping Thing

I noticed as familiarity crept into my own ministry. What are the signs of this creeping familiarity? One of the things is a failure to appreciate the pastor. You will notice how the congregation responds to visiting preachers just because it's something new.

I notice the level of response I receive when I am outside my church. I notice that the level of response I receive is higher outside my own church. The miracles are more and the receptivity is higher. This is one of the most natural phenomena in Christian churches today. Intercessory prayer is necessary to keep out these spiritual creepers. Intercessory prayer will fight that creeping familiarity that kills the flow of the Spirit.

*Chapter 22*

# How to Intercede against the Law of Things Determined

## Intercession Deals with the Law of Things Determined

Seventy weeks ARE DETERMINED upon thy people and upon thy holy city, to finish the transgression and to make an end of sins and to make reconciliation for inequity, and to bring in everlasting righteousness and to seal up the vision and prophecy, and to anoint the most Holy.

Daniel 9:24

Daniel had been praying for his people. He wanted God to move on their behalf. Suddenly, he had an angelic visitor who gave him an astonishing message. You see, Daniel was trying to bring about a change in the situation of his people. However, it was not to be so.

Daniel was informed that the divine laws of heaven had determined a seventy-week punishment for the people of God. There was nothing he could do about it. By this Scripture I am drawing your attention to what I call *determined things*. These are things that cannot be changed. They will happen whether you pray or not!

Intercessory prayer helps you to handle determined things. Do not misunderstand me; there are many things that are changeable. If they were not changeable there would be no point in praying. What I am showing you is that there are some things that are unchangeable (determined things).

War is sometimes decreed on certain nations. There is nothing you can do about it. If it is unchangeable the Lord will tell you that it is unchangeable and then He will show you what to do. Daniel was informed that seventy weeks of all sorts of punishments were definitely going to happen to Israel. There was nothing he could do about it.

Death is often one of those determined things. Look at this amazing Scripture. It tells us that there is a definite time for you to depart from this earth. Because of this, there is no need to worry about death anymore.

**Is there not an APPOINTED TIME to man upon earth?...**

**Job 7:1**

Job described the life of a man as the days of a hired servant. When the contract is over it's over.

**...are not his days also like the day of an HIRELING? [contract worker]**

**Job 7:1**

There's nothing you can do about it. The difference here is that you don't know the last day of your contract. That is why you must be ready all the time.

And that is why you must not be afraid. When intercession cannot change a determined thing, intercession shows you how to live with it or prepare for it!

Even Julius Caesar knew that! He said that death "will come when it will come."

*Cowards die many times before their deaths;*
*The valiant never taste of death but once.*
*Of all the wonders that I yet have heard,*
*It seems to me most strange that men should fear,*
*Seeing that death, a necessary end,*
*Will come when it will come.*

## Chapter 23

# How to Intercede against the Law of the Stars

## Intercession Deals with the Stars

Traditionally, born again Christians stay off the subject of stars. The Bible does not teach us to study stars or to use them for guidance. However, I want to mention what I call the influence of the stars.

I would like to show you a couple of scriptures that indicate that the stars have some influence on the events on earth. For instance, Jesus' birth was shown to the wise men from the east by a star.

**Now when Jesus was born in Bethlehem of Judaea in the days of Herod the king, behold, there came wise men from the east to Jerusalem, Saying, Where is he that is born king of the Jews? For we have seen HIS STAR in the east, and are come to worship him. ... When they had heard the king, they departed; and, lo, THE STAR, which they saw in the east, went before them, till it came and stood over where the young child was. When they saw THE STAR they rejoiced with exceeding great joy.**

**Matthew 2:1,2,9,10**

The influence or significance of stars was acknowledged in scripture in the birth of Christ. All I am trying to say is that there is some meaning and some import to these stars. It looks as though there is something arranged and determined over there.

Notice these Scriptures

**Canst thou bind THE SWEET INFLUENCES of Pleiades, or loose the bands of Orion? Canst thou bring**

**forth Mazzaroth in his season? Or canst thou guide Arcturus with his sons? Knowest thou the ordinances of heaven? Canst thou set THE DOMINION THEREOF IN THE EARTH?**

**Job 38:31-33**

The *Orion* referred to in this scripture, is the constellation of stars known as the giant.

The *Pleiades* is the name given to seven stars in the constellation Taurus.

The *Arcturus* is a constellation of stars in the northern hemisphere called the great bear.

The *Mazzaroth* are twelve signs of the zodiac.

The zodiac is a belt of the heavens including all apparent positions of the sun, moon, and planets as known to ancient astronomers, and divided into twelve equal parts (signs of the zodiac).

The Scripture above speaks of the *sweet influence* of Pleiades. This is the influence of the stars on the events on the planet earth. It asks the question, "Can thou set *the dominion thereof* in the earth?" The dominion in the earth refers to the influence and control that this constellation of stars has on the affairs of men. I believe that through the power of intercessory prayer, every negative influence of the Mazzaroth or the Pleiades will not prevail!

Perhaps you did not know that there are so many factors in play that threaten our existence. God is giving you many more reasons to become a practising intercessor. Every heavenly decree that is written in the stars against you will be changed in your favour as you intercede.

## Chapter 24

# How to Intercede about the Laws of God

## Intercession Deals with the Laws of God

The law of God speaks of God's ability to implement *judgement or mercy*. In any given situation, Almighty God has two options - judgement or mercy. However, the Bible makes it clear that God prefers the *mercy* option. God prefers showing mercy to passing judgement!

> **Who is a God like unto thee, that pardoneth iniquity, and passeth by the transgression of the remnant of his heritage? He retaineth not his anger forever, because HE DELIGHTETH [PREFERS] IN MERCY.**
>
> **Micah 7:18**

The Word teaches that God has no pleasure in the death of the wicked.

> **...as I live, saith the Lord God, I have NO PLEASURE in the death of the wicked.**
>
> **Ezekiel 33:11**

When God passes out a judgement, it is often very severe and irreversible. Because our God is a God of justice, He has no option but to pass out judgements when they are due.

Abraham and Moses are two examples of people who stood in the way of God's judgement. When Sodom and Gomorrah deserved the judgement of fire, it was Abraham who prevented the wrath of God. His intercessory prayer is the greatest example of how God listens to a man.

**Why would God listen to a mere man? God wants to have a reason to choose mercy and to avoid judgement.** Any good leader with a heart for God is always looking for an opportunity to avoid judgement and to show mercy.

**And Abraham drew near, and said, Will thou also destroy the righteous with the wicked?**

**Genesis 18:23**

Unfortunately, Abraham was not able to secure the release of Sodom and Gomorrah from God's judgement. God could not find even five righteous people in the city. The Lord tried to avoid judgement but it didn't work!

Moses, however, was able to secure deliverance for Israel.

**Therefore he said that he would destroy them, had not Moses his chosen STOOD BEFORE HIM in the breach, to turn away his wrath lest he should destroy them.**

**Psalm 106:23**

Dear minister, God has called you to stand in the breach. As you stand in between God's judgement and the people, you will save many lives. Become an intercessor! You will save nations!

## Chapter 25

# Seven Signs That Show That You Are Engaged in Travailing Prayer

My little children, of whom I TRAVAIL in birth again...

Galatians 4:19

Epaphras... always LABOURING FERVENTLY for you in prayers...

Colossians 4:12

Travailing prayer is the prayer that gives birth to new things. If you want to give birth to new dimensions in your ministry, you will have to go into travailing prayer. Stories have been told of people who engaged in travailing prayer until there were holes in the ground where they knelt to pray. Many of the revivals in times past were birthed by travailing intercessors.

Travailing prayer is the prayer that labours passionately until the baby is born. So what is travailing prayer, and how can I know whether I am engaged in travailing prayer or not? In this chapter, I want to give you some signs to look out for. These signs will tell you whether you are engaged in travailing prayer or not.

Women who have had children can best teach travailing prayer. They will describe the experience of the labour room in graphic detail! *Just as there is no baby without the labour, there will be nothing new spiritually except you labour in prayer.*

## Seven Signs of Labour Ward Prayer

**...For as soon Zion travailed [laboured] she brought forth her children.**

**Isaiah 66:7**

## 1. Long hours of prayer

Most women experience labour for several hours. After several hours of pain, the woman will give birth to a new baby. Praying for a long time gives birth to new churches and ministries.

## 2. Suffering

When women are in the labour ward they suffer all sorts of afflictions. Without the suffering, there is no breakthrough. When you engage in travailing prayer you may have to fast and sacrifice other pleasures. This is part of your labour experience. I tell you, the rewards are great!

## 3. Pain

There is a lot of pain involved in having a baby. The pain of fasting and the pain of sacrifice are part of travailing prayers.

## 4. Shame

Perhaps as you fast and pray you may not look very attractive. You may lose some weight from fasting and waiting on the Lord.

Someone once told me mockingly, "Do you think that you'll go to heaven by being a skeleton?" I had been fasting and praying for the establishment of a new fellowship. I looked like a rake and my friends mocked at me! However, I saw the birth of a new Christian fellowship and that gave me great joy. One day I will also reap my reward in heaven.

## 5. Tiredness

You can get very tired as you pray fervently. If you are lazy, you cannot engage in travailing prayer. Travailing prayer is different from Bible study and listening to tapes. It involves the physical effort of praying for hours. Moses became so tired that he had to have people hold up his hands.

## 6. Hunger

This is part of the price you pay as you wait on God. Do you think a woman in labour gets up every five minutes to have a snack? Certainly not! She endures the hunger until it is all over. Ask any woman who has had a child and she will tell you that what I am saying is true.

## 7. The New Baby

Labouring prayers always give rise to something new. As time passes, you will see that new thing in your hands and give glory to God. Perhaps it will be a new church or a new fellowship. Perhaps it will be a new phase in your ministry. It is not easy to labour in prayer, but it is worth it!

## Chapter 26

# Thirty-two Reasons Why
# I Pray in Tongues

**I thank my God, I speak with tongues more than ye all.**
**1 Corinthians 14:18**

In my opinion the ability to pray in tongues is probably the best gift that God gave to ministers. In this chapter I want to share with you why praying in tongues is very important and helpful for every minister. Each of the thirty-two reasons has a biblical foundation and I want you to think about them for your own benefit.

**For if I pray in an unknown tongue, my spirit prayeth, but my understanding is unfruitful. [My mind is a blank - TCNT]**
**1 Corinthians 14:14**

1. When I pray in tongues I charge myself up like a battery (1 Corinthians 14:4).

2. When I pray in tongues I am immediately inspired by the Holy Spirit (Acts 2:4).

3. When I pray in tongues I am praying from my heart (spirit) (1 Corinthians 14:14).

4. When I pray in tongues my prayer is dictated and directed by the Holy Spirit (Acts 2:4).

5. When I pray in tongues I operate instantly in the spirit realm (1 Corinthians 14:1).

6. When I pray in tongues other people do not understand what I am saying (1 Corinthians 14:1).

7. When I pray in tongues devils do not understand what I am saying (1 Corinthians 14:1).

8. When I pray in tongues I can hear the voice of the Spirit by interpreting my prayer (1 Corinthians 14:13).

9. When I pray in tongues I can pray for long hours like Jesus (Mark 1:35; Luke 6:12).

10. When I pray in tongues I can practise intercession for souls, families and nations (Ephesians 6:18).

11. When I pray in tongues I can speak to myself and to God. This helps me to concentrate on God everywhere I am (1 Corinthians 14:28).

12. When I pray in tongues I give thanks and praises very well (1 Corinthians 14:17).

13. When I pray in tongues it is a sign to the world that Christ is in me (Mark 16:17).

14. When I pray in tongues I have taken the first step into supernatural things (Acts 2:4).

15. When I pray in tongues I am exercising faith (Galatians 3:5).

16. When I pray in tongues I am doing what great men like Paul did (1 Corinthians 14:18; Hebrews 6:12).

17. When I pray in tongues I can pray against my enemies (in their presence) without their knowing what I am saying.

18. When I pray in tongues I can pray and think (1 Corinthians 14:14).

19. When I pray in tongues I can pray and study (1 Corinthians 14:14).

20. When I pray in tongues I can pray and read my Bible (1 Corinthians 14:14).

21. When I pray in tongues I can pray and read other books (1 Corinthians 14:14).

22. When I pray in tongues I can pray and listen to tapes (1 Corinthians 14:14).

23. When I pray in tongues I can pray and watch videos
    (1 Corinthians 14:14).

24. When I pray in tongues I can pray and have my bath
    (1 Corinthians 14:14).

25. When I pray in tongues I can pray and dress up
    (1 Corinthians 14:14).

26. When I pray in tongues I can pray and walk
    (1 Corinthians 14:14).

27. When I pray in tongues I can pray and write
    (1 Corinthians 14:14).

28. When I pray in tongues I can pray and cook
    (1 Corinthians 14:14).

29. When I pray in tongues I can pray and work in the office
    (1 Corinthians 14:14).

30. When I pray in tongues I can pray and do my hair
    (1 Corinthians 14:14).

31. When I pray in tongues I can pray and drive my car
    (1 Corinthians 14:14).

32. When I pray in tongues I can pray and wait for the bus
    (1 Corinthians 14:14).

# Part III

# VISITATION

## Chapter 27

# Twelve Reasons Why Pastors Must Visit Their Sheep

Pastors, visitation will transform your pastoral ministry! Visitation gives rise to explosive church growth. Visitation is all about going to people's homes and workplaces in order to minister to them. Ministering to people in their home settings is one of the greatest keys to an effective ministry.

Visitation is an essential part of real pastoral ministry. Visitation is not pseudo-ministry. It is the real thing. Regardless of how much you pray you must still visit the sheep. Read your Bible and you will discover that God expects pastors to visit their sheep.

Dear pastor, choose to have more than a preaching centre where the sheep gather. Do not conduct yourself as an armchair executive or a Prime Minister. Be a real shepherd who seeks the lost sheep wherever they may be found. That is real pastoral ministry.

**Therefore thus saith the Lord God of Israel against the pastors that feed my people; Ye have scattered my flock, and driven them away, and HAVE NOT VISITED THEM: behold I will visit upon you the evil of your doings, saith the Lord.**

**Jeremiah 23:2**

## Twelve Reasons Why Pastors Must Visit Their Sheep

1.  Every church member needs a visit.

2.  Every church member deserves a visit.

3.  Every church member expects a visit.

4. The more visits a sheep has, the more healthy it will be.

5. A visit makes a sheep a permanent church member.

6. God expects every pastor to visit the sheep.

7. Every sheep needs a repeated visit from the same pastor.

8. Every sheep needs visits from other pastors and shepherds.

9. The sin of neglect is the failure to visit.

10. Totally neglecting the sheep is the sin of abandonment.

11. Many of the sheep will fall away without visitation.

12. The church will not grow without visitation.

Not every problem can be solved in the church service. Many problems cannot be solved by a phone call.

When you take care of God's flock you will realize how many problems people have. The Book of Ezekiel tells us that many sheep were diseased, broken and driven away.

**The diseased have ye not strengthened, neither have ye healed that which was SICK, neither have ye bound up that which was BROKEN, neither have ye brought again that which was DRIVEN AWAY, neither have ye sought that which was lost; but with force and with cruelty have ye ruled them. And they were scattered, because there is no shepherd: and they became meat to all the beasts of the field, when they were scattered.**

**Ezekiel 34:4,5**

The preaching from the pulpit cannot solve all the problems of the sheep. Sheep must be sought out. "…neither have ye sought that which was lost." (Ezekiel 34:4).

The members of your church deserve a visit because Jesus died for them. He gave His life for them. Today, people are concerned with building their companies, businesses, houses and empires. No one cares about the sheep. Jesus asked Peter on three occasions, "Do you love me?" Peter said, "Of course I do!" That would have been our response too. But Jesus made it clear that if you love Him, you should feed His sheep.

Sometimes, people need repeated visits because one visit is not enough to solve the problem. There are times that I have visited someone and nothing happened. There were times when someone else visited the same person and there was a breakthrough!

Failure to visit the sheep is neglect! In some cases, it is actually abandonment. Do not be surprised when the wrath of God comes upon shepherds.

**Cursed be he that doeth the work of the Lord deceitfully, and cursed be he that keepeth back his sword from blood.**

**Jeremiah 48:10**

## Chapter 28

# Three Secrets behind the Power of Visitation

Visits have life-changing power! Many pastors do not know the secret behind the power of visitation. In this chapter, I want you to understand why visitation, in the ministry of a pastor, is so powerful!

## Visitation Is a Powerful Mixture of Three Forces

1. *Visitation is an expression of LOVE*

2. *Visitation involves the ministry of the WORD*

3. *Visitation involves the ministry of PRAYER*

The *Word* of God is powerful and life changing. The Bible says that it brings light where there is darkness. It is therefore no surprise that it has a powerful effect on people.

Prayer is also powerful. The Bible says that it availeth much. That means it has great effect.

But the Bible also says that *love* never fails! There are many spiritual weapons that we use all the time. No weapon has been described as "never failing". This makes love a very powerful weapon.

Sometimes, we minister the Word but the people don't feel loved. **In visitation, there is a mixture of the Word, prayer and love.** The person who is being visited feels loved. For you to have gone to his home, you must really love him! The act of journeying to someone's house at an odd hour demonstrates great love. You cannot demonstrate love in words alone.

**My little children let us not love in word, neither in tongue; but in DEED and in truth.**

**1 John 3:18**

Loving in deed involves going to people's homes. Loving in deed involves knowing the real life situations that people live in.

Sometimes the person who is being visited does not even hear the words that you speak. **What remains with him is the fact that you cared enough to come.**

Dear minister, do not underestimate the effect of this powerful mixture - the Word, love and prayer!

## Chapter 29

# Eight Guidelines for Fruitful Visitation

1.  Every visit must accomplish something

2.  Every visit must begin with a relaxing social segment

3.  Pastors must remember that shepherding visits are not social outings

4.  Every pastoral visit must be a spiritual event with a spiritual impact

5.  Every pastoral visit must include the ministering of the Word

6.  A visit becomes effective when the power of God is released through prayer

7.  Every pastoral visit must end with a powerful prayer

8.  A visit must have a powerful lasting impact

**He came unto his own... But as many as received him, to them he gave power to become the sons of God, even to them that believe on his name:**

**John 1:11,12**

Jesus accomplished a lot in His three-year visit to the earth. You will notice that Jesus did not waste time doodling in the ministry. He preached, taught and ministered to people.

The first part of Jesus' visit to the earth was a relaxing social segment. He fitted into the society and became one of their own.

**And he went down with them, and came to Nazareth, and was subject unto them: but his mother kept all these sayings in her heart. And Jesus increased in wisdom and stature, and in favour with God and man.**

**Luke 2:51,52**

But Jesus remembered that He was not just paying a social visit to the earth. He preached and blessed the people. His prayers were so powerful that they raised the dead and cast out devils. After that visit, this earth has never been the same again.

**And there are also many other things which Jesus did, the which, if they should be written every one, I suppose that even the world itself could not contain the books that should be written. Amen.**

**John 21:25**

# Chapter 30

# Ten Rules for Visitation

## 1. A pastor must never refuse a request for a visit.

It is not always that a sheep will cry for help; when they do make sure that you respond. Paul did not ignore the cry for help.

> ...There stood a man of Macedonia and prayed him, saying, Come over into Macedonia, and help us.
>
> **Acts 16:9**

## 2. Every pastor must discern the unspoken request for a visit.

Whenever a church member is in difficulty, you must discern the need for attention. The song says, "His eyes are on the sparrow". Just as His eyes are on the sparrow, your eyes must be on the sheep. Just as God has numbered your hair, you must number your sheep and look out for them. The anger of the Lord is upon the shepherds who ignore the problems of the sheep.

> The DISEASED have ye not strengthened, neither have ye healed that which was SICK, neither have ye bound up that which was BROKEN, neither have ye brought again that which was DRIVEN AWAY, neither have ye sought that which was LOST; but with force and with cruelty have ye ruled them. And they were SCATTERED, because there is no shepherd: and they became meat to all the beasts of the field, when they were scattered.
>
> **Ezekiel 34:4,5**

This scripture highlights the problems of church members: diseased, sick, broken, lost, driven away, scattered, etc. May God open your eyes to see when there is a need. May God give you the heart to care for His people.

## 3. Every pastor or shepherd must practise both routine and special circumstance visitation.

Every shepherd must have a routine for visiting his or her sheep. When I was sixteen years old I drew up a list of members in my fellowship. I decided to visit every one of them during the holidays. I drew maps to everyone's house. There was nothing particularly wrong with anyone. As a shepherd, I had decided to visit the sheep routinely.

The shepherd's heart roams the field! He wonders where everyone is. He wonders whether they are all right.

However, there are special circumstances that arise. These special circumstances such as: death, sickness, bereavement, birth of a child, marital crisis, etc. also call for extra visits.

## 4. Special circumstances in a church member's life is a call for urgent pastoral action.

**And David said unto Saul, Thy servant kept thy father's sheep and there came a lion, and a bear, and took a lamb out of the flock: And I WENT OUT AFTER HIM and smote him, and delivered it out of its mouth, and when he arose against me, I caught him by his beard, and smote him and slew him.**

**1 Samuel 17:34**

When a lion attacks the sheep, it is definitely an emergency for the shepherd. This is not a routine event. It calls for rapid action. Whenever there is a special circumstance in someone's life, the pastor must be quick to respond. Your church member may be in the mouth of a roaring lion. Just like David the shepherd, you must go out after him.

In every field of endeavour there are emergencies. Even in the field of medicine there are categorized emergencies. For instance, there are surgical emergencies, gynaecological emergencies, and so on. A doctor is trained to diagnose and react rapidly to these emergencies.

When people are broken by circumstances, it is a spiritual emergency. When people are lost and are at the mercy of wolves, it is a spiritual emergency. I can just picture a member of mine in the realm of the Spirit. I see him in the mouth of the lion. How urgently he needs help. But this is just a picture of where many sheep are.

**The DISEASED have ye not strengthened, neither have ye healed that which was SICK, neither have ye bound up that which was BROKEN, neither have ye brought again that which was DRIVEN AWAY, neither have ye sought that which was LOST; but with force and with cruelty have ye ruled them. And they were SCATTERED, because there is no shepherd: and they became meat to all the beasts of the field, when they were scattered.**

**Ezekiel 34:4,5**

In the ministry world, these special circumstances are our emergencies. We must respond rapidly if we want to save our sheep's lives.

## 5. Every pastor must practise both surprise and expected visits.

Surprise and expected visits have different effects. They are both important and must both be practised.

## 6. Surprise visits reveal the real circumstances of your church members lives.

Surprise visits often show the real state of affairs in people's homes. I have walked into people's houses and found them smoking away. At other times, I have found people living together when they were not really married. I have discovered members living in abject poverty and misery. They looked so nice and polished in church. You would never imagine the circumstances of the person's home. Surprise visits help you to know who you are pastoring. They even help you to preach and minister aright.

## 7. Expected visits give church members the chance to show their best.

When someone is expecting a visitor, he prepares the home. This enables the church members to put up their best. This gives them a sense of accomplishment as the pastor sees the best of them.

## 8. Pastors must protect themselves by visiting in pairs.

**...and send them two and two before his face into every city...**

**Luke 10:1**

Two are better than one. One strengthens the other. You help each other to preach and to share the Word. One puts to flight a thousand and two put to flight ten thousand. That is why Jesus sent them out in "twos". As you visit people of the opposite sex, they cannot easily claim that you are coming with ulterior motives because you do not come alone. This is the advantage of visiting in pairs.

## 9. It is safer for two ministers of the same sex to go on visitation.

As you frequently visit, you will find yourself bonding with your partner. You may not wish to bond with the person with whom you are doing visitation.

## 10. Pastors must not visit more than it's necessary to avoid giving the wrong impression.

**Withdraw thy foot from thy neighbours house; lest he be wary of thee and so hate thee.**

**Proverbs 25:17**

If you constantly visit a particular person, the mood of that person will change from *exhilaration* to *uncertainty* to *irritation* to *anger.* Do not let your church members hate you because you visit them too often. They will begin to wonder what your motives are. "Is the pastor hungry? Does he want some food? Does he want something from us?", they will ask themselves.

## Chapter 31

# Seven Tips That Make
# Visitation Easier

1.  **Combine your journey to and from church with a visit.**

    **...Redeeming the time...**

    **Ephesians 5:16**

I like the way someone comments about this Scripture. He says, *"Buying up those moments which others throw away."* When you buy up those moments that others throw away, you will achieve great things for God.

2.  **Combine your journey to and from work with a visit.**

    **...buy up those moments...**

    **Ephesians 5:16**

3.  **Always do multiple visits in one trip.**

    **...buy up those moments...**

    **Ephesians 5:16**

There are often a number of people who can be visited on one journey. I often try to visit several people on one journey.

4.  **Visit all the people living in the same area in one trip.**

A good pastor must know the people who live in an area. Anytime that you are in that area, you must know the potential visits you can make.

5.  **Visit people at work or in school when you cannot get them at home.**

    **See then that ye walk circumspectly... as wise...**

    **Ephesians 5:15**

Some people do not have a home that can be visited. Sometimes they are living with uncles and aunts. Sometimes they sleep outside on the street. Perhaps you can visit them at their workplaces or schools. I have made many successful visits to people in school and at work.

## 6. Use Sundays as your most valuable day for visitation.

**...Redeeming the time... [buying up those moments]**
**Ephesians 5:16**

Sundays are great days for visitation. Most people relax at home on Sunday afternoons. Make the most of your Sundays. Sundays are working days for pastors. Pastors must work on Sundays and rest on Mondays.

## 7. Do not be afraid of visiting late in the night.

Blessed are the people whom the master will find working in the second and third watches of the night. The second and third watches of the night were nine p.m. and twelve midnight respectively. This is the stamp of approval for servants who do God's work as late as 9.00 p.m. or midnight.

**...and if ye shall come in the SECOND WATCH, or in the THIRD WATCH, and find them so, BLESSED ARE THOSE SERVANTS.**
**Luke 12:38**

Many people sleep late anyway. Television keeps people awake in their homes. **There are many people you will never reach unless you visit them at a late hour.** But make sure you visit in pairs. This provides safety in case someone thinks you have the wrong motive.

## Chapter 32

# Five Visits That Have Life-Changing Power

## The Visits of Jehovah

### 1. A visit to solve marital problems

*God visited Adam and Eve*

> And they HEARD THE VOICE OF THE LORD GOD walking in the garden in the cool of the day: and Adam and his wife hid themselves from THE PRESENCE OF THE LORD God amongst the trees of the garden.
>
> **Genesis 3:8**

The Lord God visited Adam and Eve in the midst of a crisis. They were having problems because they had done something wrong. Adam was blaming Eve for talking to the serpent. Eve was blaming Adam for not spending time with her. It was a veritable marriage crisis - they didn't have clothes to wear and they didn't have any money. The Lord walked in at the right time. He showed them the consequences of their actions. He ministered the Word of God to them. Then He organised some new clothes for the family. What a visit! This visit changed the course of human history.

> Unto Adam also and to his wife did the Lord God make coats of skins, and clothed them.
>
> **Genesis 3:21**

### 2. A visit to encourage people

*God visited Abraham*

> And when Abram was ninety years old and nine, THE LORD APPEARED to Abram, and said unto him, I am the Almighty God; walk before me, and be thou perfect... THOU SHALT BE A FATHER of many

**nations. Neither shall thy name anymore be called Abram, but thy name shall be called Abraham...**

**Genesis 17:1,5**

Abraham had been married for many years and had not been able to have a child. This was a great problem for his family. During a visitation by Jehovah, a word of encouragement was spoken. You are going to be a father! Dear pastor, can you imagine the encouraging effect of those words on your life if you were in Abraham's situation?

Many times when I have visited people, they have said, "I feel so encouraged." *The combination of love, prayer and the Word is an unbeatable mixture.*

## 3. A visit to bring advice and guidance

*God visited Isaac*

**And THE LORD APPEARED unto him, and said, Go not down into Egypt; dwell in the land which I shall tell thee of:**

**Genesis 26:2**

There was an economic crisis in Isaac's city. As he prepared to get a visa to travel, he received a visitation. During the visitation he received advice. The Lord told him, "Don't travel like everyone else." God will look after you!

Isaac's life was changed forever because of that piece of advice! Many people's lives are changed forever because of a visit that brings advice. As you go out on visitation, see yourself as someone bringing advice and guidance to God's people.

## 4. A visit that makes a sheep committed, anointed and a tithe payer

*God visited Jacob*

**And Jacob awaked out of his sleep, and he said, Surely THE LORD IS IN THIS PLACE; and I knew it not.**

**Genesis 28:16**

Jacob received a visitation from the Lord. He was a backslidden person who had cheated many people. That night, his life was changed forever - a crooked person was made straight. From then on, he became a committed Christian. He decided to pay tithes and to help build the church. What a difference visitation can make. Do you see what a powerful weapon visitation is in the ministry of a pastor?

> **And Jacob vowed a vow, saying, If God will be with me, and will keep me in this way that I go, and will give me bread to eat, and raiment to put on, So that I come again to my father's house in peace; then shall the LORD be my God: And this stone, which I have set for a pillar, shall be God's house: and of all that thou shalt give me I will surely give the tenth unto thee.**
>
> **Genesis 28:20-22**

Dear friend, when you go on visitation, talk to your members about commitment. Teach them to pay their tithes. Teach them the blessings of divine protection and provisions. Your visit will have a permanent effect on their lives.

## 5. A visit to get a member's attention so God can speak to him

### *God visited Moses*

> **And the angel of THE LORD APPEARED unto him in a flame of fire out of the midst of a bush: and he looked, and, behold, the bush burned with fire, and the bush was not consumed.**
>
> **Exodus 3:2**

Moses was experiencing a "wilderness season" in his life. Things had not gone well with him for over forty years. One visit changed all of that.

Sometimes a visit by the pastor can draw the attention of a church member to the fact that God knows him personally. The impact of this is often remarkable! There is a dramatic change as people realize that God has them in mind. As it was with Moses, a long season of backsliding can end through one visit.

## Chapter 33

# Five Visits That Bring a Permanent Change

## The Visits of Jesus Christ

### 1. A visit that brings salvation to many lives

*Jesus visited the World*

> **But AS MANY AS RECEIVED HIM, to them gave he power to become the sons of God, even to them that believe on his name:**
>
> **John 1:12**

This is my favourite example of a powerful visit - three and a half years that changed the world forever. **This is the most phenomenal visit of all time. This is the mother of all visits - the visit that changed the world forever!**

Thank God that Jesus came. He could have written a letter to us. He could have sent an angel. But He came Himself. That demonstrated the love of God to mankind.

Many people have responded to this love. The fruits of this visit are everywhere. Every church building you see is a result of this visit. Every Christian you see is a fruit of this visit. Every minister of the gospel is a product of Jesus' three-and-a-half year visit to the world.

A visit can bring salvation. Christ's visit to the earth brought salvation to millions. There are many times that I have led people to Christ during a visit. I have seen some of these people permanently established in Christ. I have seen people weep as they gave their lives to Christ in their living rooms.

As you go on visitation, make sure you minister to everyone who is not saved in the household. Always remember to lead people to Christ during your visits.

## 2.  A visit that brings healing

### *Jesus visited Peter's house*

> And when JESUS WAS COME INTO PETER'S HOUSE, he saw his wife's mother laid, and sick of a fever. And he touched her hand, and the fever left her: and she arose, and ministered unto them.
>
> **Matthew 8:14,15**

During visitation, you can also pray for the sick. Believe God for the anointing to flow through you. Visitation may be your only opportunity to try out the gift of healing.

## 3.  A visit (on request) that yielded miracles

### *Jesus visited Jarius' house*

> And, behold, there came a man named Jairus, and he was a ruler of the synagogue: and he fell down at Jesus' feet, and BESOUGHT HIM THAT HE WOULD COME INTO HIS HOUSE:
>
> **Luke 8:41**

We are so used to seeing the power of God in a packed service. We think that God can only move when there are thousands of people present. Let me share a secret with you. Did you know that Jesus reserved the best miracles for the eyes of a few? Why didn't hte walk on the water before thousands of people? When He rebuked the storm, why did He do it before only twelve people who were already committed to Him? Did you know that when Jesus filled Peter's boat with so much fish it began to sink, it was only Peter, Andrew, James and John who saw it? When He rose from the dead why didn't He show Himself to thousands of people?

Dear friend, learn the mystery of godliness! *God does not need to impress anyone.* God can do the greatest miracles in the privacy of someone's home. Feel free to minister the power of God.

The first time I experienced someone falling under the power of the Holy Spirit was in a bedroom (not in a church hall). I was ministering to a young man and he collapsed under the power. There was no one there to see it happen but it was real!

As you go on visitation, get ready for God's power!

## 4. A visit that brought teaching and domestic advice

*Jesus visited Mary and Martha*

**Now it came to pass, as they went, that he entered into a certain village: and a certain woman named Martha RECEIVED HIM INTO HER HOUSE.**

**Luke 10:38**

Jesus practised all kinds of visits. He visited two ladies and gave them good domestic advice. He told Martha that she was too involved in the kitchen. In other words, He advised her to become more spiritual.

It is not everything you can comment about in someone's home. If you have the right relationship with the person you may be able to speak. If not, keep your mouth shut and move on! You may get into trouble by speaking about things you have no business commenting on.

**...A fool uttereth all his mind...**

**Proverbs 29:11**

## 5. A visit for general interaction and direct rebukes

*Jesus visited a Pharisee*

**And as he spake, a certain Pharisee besought him to dine with him: AND HE WENT IN, AND SAT DOWN TO MEAT.**

**Luke 11:37**

The Lord visited all kinds of people and therefore you must visit all kinds of people. When He visited this Pharisee, there were a lot of rebukes. Jesus was not intimidated by the dinner that was set before him, neither should you be.

> **And when the Pharisees saw it, he marvelled that he had not first washed before dinner. And the Lord said unto him, Now do ye Pharisees make clean the outside of the cup and the platter; BUT YOUR INWARD PART IS FULL OF RAVENING AND WICKEDNESS, YE FOOLS...**
>
> **Luke 11:38**

This visit turned out into one of the strongest rebukes that Jesus ever meted out to hypocrites. Jesus told His hosts that they were fools.

## Chapter 34

# Five Visits That Establish
# Church Members

## The Pauline Visits

### 1. A visit that leads to the Holy Spirit baptism

*Paul visited the Ephesus Christians*

> And it came to pass, that, while Apollos was at Corinth, Paul having passed through the upper coasts CAME TO EPHESUS: AND FINDING CERTAIN DISCIPLES, And when Paul had laid his hands on them, the Holy Ghost came on them and they spake with tongues and prophesied.
>
> **Acts 19:1,6**

Do not hesitate to minister the baptism of the Holy Spirit when you are on visitation. **A visiting minister is a mobile church service.** Good things can happen when you are anointed of the Spirit. I remember ministering the baptism of the Holy Spirit in someone's home. This person was so happy. He continued speaking in tongues for over one hour. If I had waited for this fellow to come to church, he may never had had the power of the Holy Spirit.

### 2. Visitation to build a relationship

*Paul visited the church at Tyre*

> ...and LANDED AT TYRE: for there the ship was to unlade her burden. And finding disciples, we tarried there seven days... And when we had ACCOMPLISHED THOSE DAYS, we departed...
>
> **Acts 21:3-5**

Sometimes a visit must be made to build a relationship. It is important for a pastor to build relationships with all or some of his church members. Visitation is one of the effective ways for building relationships. Paul had no other reason than to accomplish certain days at certain places.

## 3.  A visit to recruit pastors

### *Paul visited Derbe and Lystra*

**THEN CAME HE TO DERBE AND LYSTRA: and, behold, a certain disciple was there named Timotheus, the son of a certain woman... Him would Paul have to go forth with him...**

**Acts 16:1,3**

Amazing things can happen during visitation. It was during visitation that Paul identified a potential pastor. Who was this pastor? It turned out to be Timothy. If Paul had not done the visit to Derbe and Lystra, some people would not have had a pastor and the Book of Timothy would never have been written.

Some years ago, I remember visiting a family that lived two hours away from the church. As I set out, I had no idea what that visit would lead to. Today, I have a whole church that is pastored by someone who joined the church as a result of that visit. I have also recruited a "Timothy" during a visit. I see you recruiting pastors as you go on visitation!

## 4.  A visit to strengthen church members

### *Paul visited Galatia and Phrygia*

**And after he had spent some time there, he departed, and WENT OVER ALL THE COUNTRY OF GALATIA AND PHRYGIA in order, strengthening all the disciples.**

**Acts 18:23**

Thank God for the life of the apostle Paul. Can you see how many different places and people he visited? If he had not done this work, what would have become of the church? Every time you go on a visit, you strengthen the sheep. Jesus smiles on you lovingly as you strengthen His little lambs.

## 5. A visit to exhort the Church

### *Paul visited Macedonia and Greece*

> **...Paul called unto him the disciples, and embraced them, and departed for to go into Macedonia. And when he had gone over those parts, and had given them MUCH EXHORTATION, he came into GREECE, And there abode three months...**
>
> Acts 20:1-3

Paul, the classic shepherd, visited Macedonia and Greece. Sometimes you can visit an entire household. You do not have to visit only one person. Notice how much exhortation was administered during this visit.

Don't forget to share the Word every time you visit. The Word is powerful! It changes lives! It is different from philosophy and wise sounding ideas. Stay with the Word even on visitation! Follow the example of Paul and be an exhorter while on visitation.

# Part IV

# TEACHING

## Chapter 35

# Fifteen Keys to Becoming a Successful Teacher of the Word

And I will give you pastors according to mine own heart which shall feed you with knowledge and understanding.

Jeremiah 3:15

### 1. Be in a state of constant preparation.

You may be called upon to preach at any time. When you are aware of this reality you will always be in tune.

### 2. Have your quiet time every day.

Most of my messages have come from my personal quiet time which I have everyday. If you are a minister and do not have a quiet time everyday, your foundation is weak.

### 3. Read books all the time.

You must have a book that you are reading. I always have one book or other that I am reading all the time. They are often unrelated to what I am preaching about. This helps me to be in a state of constant preparation.

### 4. Listen to tapes all the time.

I always have a set of tapes that I am listening to. This is what I mean by a state of constant preparation. Sometimes, people wonder how I am able to cope with several preaching duties at the same time. I am able to do this because I am in a state of constant preparation.

### 5. Base every sermon on the Scriptures.

Stay with the mainstream of the Gospel. The Bible is your main textbook. Let it be the rock upon which you base your ministry. Do not replace the gold of the Word with the brass of secular teachings.

## 6. Have a clear purpose for every message.

What are you trying to achieve? Do you want to get people saved or healed? Having a clear purpose will guide you as to what to say.

## 7. Give the right kind of title to your message

There are three main types of titles: *Evangelistic titles, Exhortational titles* and *Teaching titles.*

***Evangelistic titles*** are dramatic sounding titles. They are intended to jolt the congregation. They sometimes bring fear into the hearts of sinners. Examples of these are:

- "Rain, rain go away"

- "You are entitled to your own opinion"

- "Silence in Heaven"

- "Judgement Day 1,2 and 3"

- "They went to hell"

***Exhortational titles*** are short, catchy phrases. These are intended to encourage the congregation. Examples of these are:

- "Daughter, you can make it"

- "Daughter you have tender eyes"

- "Woman, thou art loosed"

- "Can I wash my hands?"

***Teaching titles*** give a clear message. They usually show a number of steps, principles or keys. **You can convert any exhortational message into a teaching message by giving it the right title.** You can have several different teaching sermons out of one exhortation. Let us do a little exercise and convert an exhortational message (Woman, thou art loosed) into a teaching message.

- "Three *steps* to becoming a woman who is loosed"

- "Seven *principles* to becoming a woman who is loosed"

- "Four *reasons* why you should be a woman who is loosed"

- " Ten *benefits* of being a woman who is loosed"

- "Six *laws* of the woman who is loosed"

- "Seven *ways* you can become a woman who is loosed"

- "Five *mistakes* of a woman who is loosed"

- "Ten *things* every Christian should know about the woman who is loosed"

- "What it means to be a woman who is loosed"

- "Twenty-five *keys* to becoming a woman who is loosed"

- "Four *phases* in the life of a woman who is loosed"

- "Eighteen *methods* by which you can become a woman who is loosed"

- "Twelve *secrets* of a woman who is loosed"

- "Eleven *strategies* of a woman who is loosed"

- "How you can become a woman who is loosed"

- "Seven *signs* of a woman who is loosed"

- "Four *symptoms* of a woman who needs to be loosed"

You can make this a formula to help you produce more organised teaching messages. You first of all choose any number of points you want. Then pick the right word (whether principles, laws, keys, secrets) to go with it. You will discover that your teaching ministry will jump to another level when you have the right kind of title.

## 8. There must be order in the sermon.

An easy way to ensure order in your message is to preach in points. You can teach in three, five, seven or as many points as you want. Let people see the progression that you are following. Remember this: if you are preaching a one-off sermon, three points are often adequate. The maximum for a one-off sermon should be seven points. If you try to teach 25 points in one sermon, you will certainly run into difficulties.

## 9. Conclude your sermon on a high note.

## 10. Do not preach for too long or too short.

## 11. Never preach without windows (illustrations, stories, parables, etc.).

A message without illustrations and personal examples is like a building without a window. Jesus never taught without illustrations and windows. The story of the prodigal son, the story of the man who was attacked on the way to Jericho and the story of the Lazarus and the rich man are vivid examples of this style of teaching. Children never forget these stories and neither do adults. The greater your teaching ministry the more like Jesus' it will be.

## 12. Always do an altar call for salvation.

The main thrust of the kingdom of God is to bring souls to Christ. We do a great disservice to the Gospel when we fail or forget to invite people to Jesus.

## 13. Stay with revelation.

Preach about things that God has given you a revelation of. If you just preach somebody's sermon without having a personal revelation of it, you will make no impact! You may actually look foolish! Avoid complex things that you do not understand. There is enough to preach about without getting stuck on difficult terrain!

## 14. Head for the anointing.

As you preach frequently, you will know when the preaching anointing comes upon you. You will also know what to do to make the anointing flow during the sermon.

Two keys to preaching in the anointing are:

i.  You must learn to break icy atmospheres and enter the anointing by openly speaking a few phrases in tongues.

ii. Staying with revelation also releases the anointing for preaching. Move from dryness into anointed preaching by sharing things that you have a personal revelation about.

## 15. Look for the five signs of the anointing when you are preaching. Preaching with the anointing is characterised by five important signs.

a.  It is preaching with authority (Mark 1:22)

b.  It is preaching with life-changing effects (Acts 4:4)

c.  It is preaching which causes crowds to gather (Mark 1:32)

d.  It is direct and cuts to the heart (Acts 2:37)

e.  It is relevant (Luke 13:4,5)

## Chapter 36

# Four Reasons Why Every Pastor Should See the Congregation as God's Garden

**For we are labourers together with God: YE ARE GOD'S HUSBANDRY [GARDEN, FARM, FIELD], Ye are God's building.**

**1 Corinthians 3:9**

Every pastor should see the congregation as God's garden, God's field or God's farm. When you see the congregation as God's farm, it will help you understand what the ministry of preaching and teaching does. When you are preaching, you are actually pouring seeds into God's farm. The type of seeds you pour into the ground determines the type of harvest you are going to get.

- **Every pastor must see himself as a farmer who plants seeds with every sermon.**

Once you understand this revelation, you will know that there is no mystery to the type of congregation you have. If you have a congregation of soul winners, it is the harvest you have earned for yourself. Every farmer gets what he plants. If you plant corn, you will get a harvest of corn. If you plant pineapples, you will harvest pineapples.

The pastor is the farmer. The congregation is a garden. Whenever the pastor preaches, he is planting a particular kind of seed. **He will have a harvest that corresponds to the type of seeds he has planted.**

It is no wonder that some churches are full of prosperous successful people. This is because their pastor teaches prosperity and success on a regular basis. Some churches are full of missionary minded people. This is because the pastor preaches about missionary work all the time.

Some churches preach about miracles. It is no wonder that miracles take place in those churches. Some pastors teach about church growth and they experience it.

Dear pastor, is it a mystery if a farmer reaps a harvest of tomatoes? Certainly not! He must have planted tomatoes! What are you planting in God's garden? Are you preaching poverty, fear and failure? Or are you preaching victory, prosperity and faith?

- **There are short-term harvests of the Word.**

What do I mean by short-term harvests? During each service, whatever you preach is a seed for a short-term harvest. If you preach a sermon of doubt and fear, you will not reap a harvest of miracles. If you preach about salvation, you will get people saved.

## I Saw the Harvest

I remember preaching at a crusade. As I taught about salvation, there was a calm response from the audience. They listened earnestly to the message of salvation. At a point, I began to speak about healing. I told the crowd that God would heal them. There was an almost immediate response from the congregation! Cripples came out of wheelchairs and the sick began to get healed as I spoke about healing.

At that moment, I was reaping a short-term harvest. I had spoken about miracles and I was reaping a harvest of miracles.

I used to think that if God was God, He should move in the same way after every sermon. However, as I have grown in the ministry, I have realized that it is not so. The reality that we are God's garden has dawned on me. If I want to have a miracle service, then I must teach about miracles and healing. I know that the congregations listening to me are God's field.

If you are not surprised when the farmer next door reaps a harvest of wheat, then do not be surprised if Benny Hinn reaps a harvest of miracles in his ministry. He preaches about miracles all the time. It is only in order that he should reap a harvest of healing from God's garden.

- **There are long-term harvests of the Word.**

Without knowing what I was doing, I sowed certain seeds in God's garden. I have taught about loyalty and I have reaped a harvest of loyal people from the garden! I have preached about the ministry and missionary work. As the years have gone by, God has blessed me with many workers and missionaries.

- **You must believe in the principle of God's garden.**

This principle will guide you into preaching the right things. Do not be in a hurry to reap a harvest. There is always a period of time between sowing and reaping. From this time onwards, carefully select what you will speak about in your church. Preach about what you want and not about what you have! As the years go by, you will realise that you have a congregation of people that are exact products of your teaching.

*Chapter 37*

# Seven Reasons Why a Pastor Should Teach in Series

Some pastors have a new sermon every Sunday. They come up with an inspiring, exhortation every week. This is commendable. However, the sheep cannot live on inspiration! They need regular, sustained and balanced teaching. If your church is to grow, you will have people staying in your church for many years. You have to have something to give them on a regular basis. This is why I believe that you must teach in series. Of course, there are times that you must give inspirational messages that are not in series. Here are seven reasons why you must learn to teach in series.

- Preaching in series is the best way to *sustain a congregation of regular attendees.* Since you will have the same people listening to you every week, you need to have an appropriate message.

- Preaching in series *is easier for the pastor* than preaching a different message every week. This is because a series is actually one message that has been broken down into little sermons. The preparation for one long sermon lasts for a long time and can be released to the sheep in stages.

- Preaching in series makes *the members have something to look forward to* the following week. It creates an air of expectation.

- Preaching in series *makes the members come back* week after week because they want to hear the conclusion of the series. This improves the attendance in church.

- Preaching in series is the only way *to cover lengthy but important topics* that must be taught in the church. For instance, it is not possible to cover all that must be taught about marriage in forty-five minutes.

- Preaching in series enables the pastor *to shorten the services* to a reasonable length of time. The pastor is not under so much stress to say everything in one week. He knows that he will have the opportunity to complete his message next week.

- Preaching in series *establishes a bond* between the pastor and his congregation. They depend on him for a regular meal. You are always attached to the people who feed you regularly!

## Chapter 38

# Four Keys to Augment Your Teaching Ministry

Perhaps your teaching ministry needs a boost. You can go higher. Let me share with you four steps that will move you on to the next level.

1. **Preach without notes.** It is much more impressive to preach extemporaneously than to be seen reading out of notes. Even if you have notes (like I do), do not appear to depend on them for every sentence you say.

2. **Practice teaching without notes by memorizing three cardinal points with three cardinal scriptures and three cardinal 'windows'.** Windows are life's examples, illustrations and stories. When you are preaching extemporaneously, it is easier to remember three main points rather than ten main points. These three points will naturally link themselves up to three scriptures and three 'windows'.

3. **Constantly soak in teaching tapes** that are unrelated to your Sunday sermons. Start preparing for preaching opportunities a year in advance.

4. **Teach regularly.** You must have a weekly opportunity to minister the Word. Anyone who preaches regularly is bound to improve. If you preach only once in a while, your preaching ministry will always remain at a low level.

## Chapter 39

# Seven Reasons Why Listening to Tapes Will Transform Your Preaching Ministry

So then faith cometh by HEARING AND HEARING by the word of God.

**Romans 10:17**

### 1. Listening to tapes will help you to know the Word of God.

Every minister needs to have an in-depth knowledge of the Word of God. An easy way to memorize the Word of God is by listening to tapes. You will hear the preacher quoting scriptures and this will help you remember the Word.

### 2. Listening to tapes will help you to soak in the voice of God.

As you soak in tapes you will receive direction for your ministry. There are always several messages within a message. As a pastor, you will hear God speaking to you about different things concerning your ministry.

### 3. Listening to tapes will help you to stay in the presence of God.

Once the Word of God is being preached, an anointed atmosphere is created. Every pastor must endeavour to remain in such an atmosphere because he may be called upon to minister at any time.

**Preach the word; be instant in season out of season; reprove, rebuke, exhort with all longsuffering and doctrine.**

**2 Timothy 4:2**

## 4. Listening to tapes will help you to catch the anointing.

As Peter preached, the Spirit fell on the congregation (Acts 10:44). Most definitely, as the Word of God is coming forth, the anointing is falling. The more you listen to tapes, the more you will be anointed (See my book on Catch the Anointing).

## 5. Listening to tapes will help you to develop a unique style of preaching.

As you listen to tapes, you will develop a unique style of preaching. It is important for you to develop a distinctive style of preaching as this will appeal to the people God has called you to. As the saying goes, "Different strokes for different folks." Not everyone will be attracted to your ministry. But God has definitely raised you up for a people.

## 6. Listening to tapes will help you to acquire general information that a minister needs.

There are many side-benefits to listening to tapes. You will always glean a lot of useful information as you soak in tapes. It is nicer to listen to a preacher who is knowledgeable about many areas of life. For instance, a good knowledge of history, politics, science, medicine, law, geography, literature and economics greatly enhance the delivery of a message.

## 7. Listening to tapes will help you to have a constant unintentional training for the ministry.

The training of a minister revolves around the Word of God. As you soak in the Word, you constantly receive some counsel. What a blessing to receive counsel without even asking for it.

## Chapter 40

# How to Establish a Doctrine in the Church

When the sower went out to sow, only one out of four seeds flourished in good ground. The Bible teaches us that the Word of God was that seed (Mark 4:14). If only a quarter of the congregation responds properly to a message, it means that you have to preach that message several times before it becomes established.

**When a subject is occasionally preached in a church, it does not lead to that doctrine being established in the congregation.** It is important to establish certain truths in the congregation so that the church can be perfected. Perfection will not come if the principles and doctrines are not established.

**Therefore leaving the principles of the doctrine of Christ, let us go on unto perfection...**
**Hebrews 6:1**

If your congregation is still struggling with the concept of church leadership, you have a problem. If your congregation still struggles with the concept of tithing, your income will be skimpy. Dear friend, how can you move on to greater things if the foundational doctrines are not established?

Let me share with you six steps that will establish a doctrine in your church. These steps are based on a simple Scripture.

**That in the mouth of two or three witnesses EVERY WORD [DOCTRINE] MAY BE ESTABLISHED.**
**Matthew 18:16**

Where there are two or more preachers saying the same thing, a doctrine will be established. Any church, which has all the ministers saying the same thing, is blessed! The Word of God will go forth with strength when it is taught over and over again.

# Six Steps That Will Establish a Doctrine in Your Church

1. **Teach a series about the subject in question**

2. **Teach another series on a sister topic.**

   For instance, if you teach about prayer you could also teach about fasting.

3. **Teach the same subject a second time.**

4. **Later on, get your assistants to teach on the same topic.**

5. **Yet again, instruct your cell leaders or shepherds to teach the same thing on another occasion.**

6. **Get visiting ministers to teach the same topic to your congregation**

   When the senior pastor, his associates, other leaders and even visiting ministers teach a doctrine, that doctrine is bound to be established.

   Sometimes I am invited to teach on loyalty but I know that one sermon is not going to change a culture of disloyalty into one of loyalty. The message must be preached over and over until it is established. **The mouth of two or more messages will establish the doctrine!** Some things will need more than a year of constant teaching before they will be established.

*Chapter 41*

# Nine Reasons Why Pastors Should Preach the Word of God

1.  **When you preach the Word of God your church members will have direction for their lives.**

    **All scripture is given by inspiration of God, and is profitable for doctrine, for reproof, for correction, for instruction in righteousness: That the man of God may be perfect, throughly furnished unto all good works.**

    **2 Timothy 3:16,17**

The Bible contains the written Word of God. It is a reliable source of direction for us all. The Word of God is given to us for direction in our lives. Everything we do must be according to the Word of God. In a very general way, the Word of God is the perfect guidebook for our lives. The Bible is a unique book that contains instruction on every possible issue that may arise. There are many that think that the Bible is not a practical and relevant book for today.

One lady told me that she believed she could practice fornication because the Bible was out of fashion. Three years later, when her boyfriend of many years ditched her, she suddenly realized that the Bible was not so archaic after all.

*The Scripture is profitable, useful, relevant and practical for every Christian today!* There are many Christians who do not want you to open the Bible; they just want a prophecy or a word of knowledge.

2.  **When you preach the Word, the congregation will have light for their darkness.**

    **Thy word is a lamp unto my feet and a light unto my path.**

    **Psalm 119:105**

There is so much darkness in the world. We often do not know what to do, but God has provided a light for Christians. What is this light that God has provided for Christians?

Thy Word is a light for my path and a lamp to my feet. God's Word is a lamp and a light for us. It is only when you put on the light that you know where to go. It is only when you put on the light that you can prevent yourself from stumbling over furniture. Jesus Christ called Himself the light of this world.

**...I am the light of the world: he that followeth me shall not walk in darkness, but shall have THE LIGHT OF LIFE.**

**John 8:12**

You need light in this life! Jesus (the Word) is the light for your life. People who have tried to live their lives without Christ and the Word have discovered that it is painful to stumble around in the darkness.

A young man approached me and informed me that he was having terrible problems in his marriage. He wanted me to help him. He wanted to know the way out of his marital difficulties. As I talked with him, I realized that what he needed was the Word.

But he said to me, "Are you going to pray for me to have my deliverance?"

I asked, "Why do you need deliverance?"

He answered, "Oh, it has been detected that my wife has a marine spirit."

I asked him, "What is a marine spirit?"

He said, "Oh, it's something they say I have to be delivered from. So I want you to deliver me."

I thought to myself, "This man wants a quick fix. He does not want the Word. He does not know that nothing sets you free like the Word of God does."

**And ye shall know the truth, and THE TRUTH SHALL MAKE YOU FREE.**

**John 8:32**

I continued to question him, "Are you a born-again Christian?"

"Yes I am."

"Are you faithful to your wife?" I asked.

He smiled, "Um… not really."

"Actually," he continued, "I have not been faithful to her at all!"

I advised this man to have a pastor and belong to a church. I told him, "Your marine spirit is the least of your problems. What you need is the Word of God to guide you in this life. You need the *light of life*, otherwise, you will continue to grope in darkness."

There are people who wonder how I know the things I preach. I remember arriving in Johannesburg for a convention. I was met by a South African delegation. When they saw me one of them asked, "Are you the Bishop?"

I said, "Yes I am."

"Really! We were expecting someone much older!

We have listened to your tapes and read your books. Somehow, we thought you were a much older person."

When you have the Word of God, your wisdom will be beyond your age. You will seem to be maturer than people of your age group.

3. **When you preach the Word of God the church members will be wise.**

**Thou through thy commandments hast made me wiser than mine enemies…I have more understanding than all my teachers: for thy testimonies are my meditation.**

**Psalm 119:98,99**

Dear pastor, do you want to have wise church members? Do you want to have stable intelligent people in your congregation? Then preach the Word of God. The Word of God will make you wise in this life. Advice and direction for business are found in the Word of God. There is more instruction for a businessperson in the Word of God than in any teaching on business management. There is more relevant practical knowledge on philosophy, political science, literature and history in the Bible than in any other book I know.

## 4. When you preach the Word of God the church members will know what to do.

I sometimes smile when people say, "God has called them to do such-and-such for Him." **If you do not obey the simple instructions in the Word, do you think that God is going to give you a greater instruction?** He that is faithful in little is faithful in much. If you do not obey the Word of God that says to pay your tithes and offerings, do you think God is going to speak to you about other things?

> **He hath shewed thee, O man, what is good; and what doth the Lord require of thee...**
>
> **Micah 6:8**

God will minister His Word through pastors and shepherds. That is why it is important to have a good church and a pastor who teaches the Word of God.

## 5. When you preach the Word of God Christians will know and understand what is happening in their lives.

In the last days, God is giving pastors who will feed us with knowledge and understanding. Receive the knowledge and understanding that God is giving you through your pastors now!

> **And I will give you pastors according to my heart, which shall feed you with knowledge and understanding.**
>
> **Jeremiah 3:15**

Apart from knowledge and understanding, God will use a man of God to give instructions to Christians. These instructions help us to become better people in life. There are times your pastor will give a commandment to fast and pray. It is important to follow these instructions. The Bible teaches that we should obey those that have spiritual authority over us.

**Obey them that have the rule over you, and submit yourselves: for they watch for your souls...**

**Hebrews 13:7**

Church members must listen to the voice of their shepherds. God has delegated the destiny of the sheep to the shepherd. God will bless your life and lead you through the voice of your shepherd. Jesus is the good overall shepherd and He told Peter to look after the sheep. That means that He was delegating the care of His sheep to under-shepherds. Dear pastors, we have an awesome responsibility and we can only do it by *staying* with the Word.

**...and the sheep follow him: for they know his voice. And a stranger they will not follow, but will flee from him: for they know not the voice of strangers.**

**John 10:4**

6. **When you preach the Word of God, sin is burned out of the congregation.**

Do you want to have a congregation of sinners? Do you want to have a congregation of immoral people, prostitutes, drug dealers, liars, thieves and murderers? I hope not!

It may sound strange to you but I have seen congregations like that. By preaching the Word of God, you ignite a fire that burns up sin.

**...I will make MY WORDS IN THY MOUTH FIRE, and this people wood, AND IT SHALL DEVOUR them.**

**Jeremiah 5:14**

**Is it not my word like as a FIRE?...**

**Jeremiah 23:29**

7. **When you preach the Word of God it knocks sense into stubborn people.**

   **...it not my word... like a HAMMER that breaketh the rock in pieces?**
                                                    **Jeremiah 23:29**

   There are always stubborn people who need to attend the school of hard knocks. Preaching the Word knocks sense into stubborn people.

8. **When you preach the Word of God people will be genuinely saved.**

   **For I am not ashamed of the gospel of Christ: for it is the power of God unto salvation to every one that believeth...**
                                                    **Romans 1:16**

   When the Word of God is not preached people are not genuinely saved. They may be members of the church but they will not be sincerely saved. Salvation is a product of the Word of God being preached. Secular teachings on success do not have the power of salvation!

9. **When you preach the Word of God you deal with the innermost thoughts of the congregation.**

   There are many people who do not express their innermost thoughts. You never know what they are thinking. They are often evasive and do not answer questions directly. It is only God's Word that can get to their hearts and minister to them!

   **For the word of God is quick, and powerful, and sharper than any two-edged sword, piercing even to the dividing asunder of soul and spirit, and of the joints and marrow, and IS A DISCERNER OF THE THOUGHTS AND INTENTS OF THE HEART.**
                                                    **Hebrews 4:12**

## Chapter 42

# Seven Reasons Why You Should Teach Your Leaders

I believe that every pastor should have special sessions with his leaders. Teaching leaders is one of the most productive activities a pastor can engage in.

*When you teach leaders, you generate sons and daughters in the ministry.* Do you realise that two of the most important letters in the New Testament were written to a leader? 1st and 2nd Timothy are books that were written to a pastor. These teachings were not intended for the benefit of the whole church. They were the Apostle Paul's teachings to his junior pastor, Timothy.

Pastors and leaders need to be taught. They need to be *separated* from the rest of the congregation in order to receive special teachings. I do this all the time and it has yielded hundreds of sons and daughters in the ministry. It has raised up pastors and shepherds all over the world.

If you do not have special regular sessions with your leaders, your church will not have the right kind of workers. Church growth will be stunted when leaders are not trained specially. Dear friend, find out what there is to teach and begin to train your leaders yourself. Perhaps this is the key that your church needs.

**THOU THEREFORE, MY SON, be strong in the grace that is in Christ Jesus. And the things that thou hast heard of me among many witnesses, the same commit thou to faithful men, who shall be able to teach others also.**

**2 Timothy 2:2**

# Seven Reasons Why You Should Teach Your Leaders

1. When you preach to leaders you are actually preaching to many more people. You are also teaching the followers of this leader.

2. Pastors must know the principle of explosive growth: *If you want GROWTH, teach your members but if you want EXPL OSIVE GROWTH, teach your leaders!*

3. *Teaching leaders establishes authority over the leaders who work under you.* This is because the authority over the leaders is demonstrated by your ability to feed them.

4. Teaching ordinary members is an investment into the church of today. *Teaching leaders is an investment into the future.* The leaders you teach will carry on into the future when you are gone. Success without a successor is failure!

5. *Every pastor must teach leaders because Jesus Christ taught leaders all the time.* Pastors must spend more time teaching leaders than teaching ordinary church members. This is the pattern set by Christ Jesus.

6. *Teaching leaders is your greatest key to true expansion.* You will not have anyone to delegate if you have not trained leaders.

7. *Every pastor must teach his leaders because the leaders will never know what to do unless you teach them.* Many pastors assume that the potential leaders around them will acquire vital knowledge by osmosis. People feel that leadership is for special people who are born that way. Osmosis is not the key to leadership - teaching is!

## Chapter 43

# Why You Must Avoid "Pseudo Word" and  Doctrines of Devils

**Now the Spirit speaketh expressly, that in the latter times some shall depart from the faith, giving heed to seducing spirits and DOCTRINES OF DEVILS...**
1Timothy 4:1

## Doctrines of Devils

When you preach the Word of God you avoid the mistake of deviating into false doctrine or "pseudo Word" teachings. Openly false doctrines are easy to spot. You can tell them a mile away!  Doctrines of groups like Jehovah Witnesses and Mormons are well known examples of erroneous doctrines. Most Christians have no difficulties spotting these things. Most pastors would not preach such flagrant error.

### "Pseudo Word"

The real danger lies in what I call 'pseudo Word' teachings. 'Pseudo Word' teachings come about because of seducing spirits. These seducing spirits lure ministers into enticing areas of ministry.

Pastors are often enticed into exciting areas of debate. There are many social causes that need a champion. **There are many political and moral issues that need a spokesman.** The question every pastor must ask himself is, "Did God call me to champion a social cause?  **Am I supposed to leave the foundational doctrines of the Word of God and move into these 'grey' areas?**" I call them 'grey' areas because it is uncertain whether they are secular topics or spiritual topics. If your call is to stay in the 'grey' areas, God will bless you over there. If not, then you have been seduced and enticed by a clever devil. Every pastor must be careful about the doctrine he is teaching.

**TAKE HEED UNTO THYSELF AND UNTO THY DOCTRINE; continue in them: for in doing this thou shalt both save thyself and them that hear thee.**

**1 Timothy 4:16**

Pseudo Word' teachings are often teachings about good things or good causes. **Something may be a good cause but that does not make it the Word of God.**

Let me show you some examples of these 'pseudo Word' doctrines. *'Pseudo Word' teachings include things like secular leadership training, secular wisdom teachings, secular success teachings, political discourses, social campaigns about social and moral issues. There are many topics such as gender issues, race and colour issues that stir up passion.* These things in themselves are not evil. The only problem with them is that they are not the central doctrines of the Bible.

I am not saying that it is wrong to preach on these issues. I am sure that God has called some people to address these things. However, you must know that these are not the foundational doctrines of the Bible. They are not the mainstream of the Word of God. They are not the gospel and they do not have the power of God unto salvation! (Romans 1:16). Make sure that you do not swerve away from the mainstream of preaching God's Word. It is the Gospel that has the power to save! Secular success teachings do not have power to save souls.

Dear friend, if God has not called you to address these topics and you make them your emphasis, I am sorry to say that you have swerved aside into fruitless ministry.

**…From which some HAVING SWERVED have turned aside unto vain jangling.**

**1 Timothy 1:6**

As far as heaven is concerned, you may have turned aside into vain jangling (worthless noise making).

**And they shall turn away their ears from the truth, and SHALL BE TURNED UNTO FABLES.**

**2 Timothy 4:4**

# Part V

# INTERACTION

*Chapter 44*

# Eight Reasons Why Interaction Is Important for Every Church

Interaction is an important part of ministry where the pastor makes personal contact with the people and establishes an important connection between himself and the congregation. He engages in informal discussions and establishes personal relationships with all sorts of people. Interaction is a key 'outside-the-pulpit' ministry that must be fully developed in order to achieve church growth.

## Eight Reasons Why Interaction Is Important for Every Church

### 1. Interaction makes people stay in the church.

Dear pastor do not forget this! People may join the church for various reasons. However, people stay in a church because of the people they know and the friends they make! This is what I call *church cement.* If you want your church to grow, interact with the members and encourage them to interact with one another!

### 2. Interaction makes people feel important.

Every soul is important! In fact, every hair on the head of every soul is important. When the Lord told us that He was numbering the hairs on our heads, He was telling us that we are very important to Him. It is important for people to feel that they are important. Personal interaction is the key to making people feel important.

**But even the very hairs of your head are all numbered...**

**Luke 12:7**

### 3. Interaction makes people feel that they are not just a number or a statistic.

Jesus said that He had not lost any of the sheep the Father had given Him. Everyone is important to God! Not even one person must be lost! No one is just a number. No one must be treated as a mere statistic. Interaction is the key to ensuring this.

### 4. Interaction makes people feel that they are not objects being used to make the pastor famous.

**In the multitude of people is the king's honour: but in the want of people is the destruction of the prince.**

**Proverbs 14:28**

People know that where there are large crowds, the pastor (king), is honoured. Sometimes the people feel that they are being used to make the pastor famous. Personal interaction will prevent church members from thinking in that way.

### 5. Interaction is important because personal contact changes wrong impressions!

The queen of Sheba had a wrong impression about who Solomon was. However, after having a personal interaction with him, she changed her mind. She was so impressed with king Solomon. She said, "You are better and greater than I thought you were."

**And she said to the king, It was a true report which I heard in mine own land of thine acts and of thine wisdom: Howbeit I believe not their words until I came, and mine eyes have seen it: And, behold, the one half of the greatness of thy wisdom was not told me: FOR THOU EXCEEDEST THE FAME THAT I HEARD.**

**2 Chronicles 9:5,6**

I have had several people telling me about the negative impressions they had about me before they knew me personally. Some people could not believe that I was so different from what

I was portrayed to be. Interaction kills wrong impressions very quickly indeed!

## 6. Interaction is important because personal contact helps people to become more committed.

Perhaps you have tried to get certain people committed to your church by preaching hard from the pulpit. Personal interaction with them may be the key that will turn them into committed members. When Jesus interacted with Nathanael on the beach it resulted in a life commitment. Notice Jesus' personal interaction with Nathanael and how it made him a committed disciple.

**Jesus saw Nathanael coming to him, and saith of him, Behold an Israelite indeed, in whom is no guile! Nathanael saith unto him, Whence knowest thou me? Jesus answered and said unto him, Before that Philip called thee, when thou wast under the fig tree, I saw thee. Nathanael answered and saith unto him, Rabbi, thou art the Son of God; thou art the King of Israel.**

**John 1:47-49**

## 7. Interaction is important because Jesus interacted.

Jesus is our great example setter. We can best learn about ministry by following his example. I want to do what Jesus did. I want to be more like Jesus.

**Now as HE WALKED BY THE SEA OF GALILEE, HE SAW SIMON AND ANDREW his brother casting a net into the sea: for they were fishers. And JESUS SAID UNTO THEM, Come ye after me, and I will make you to become fishers of men.**

**Mark 1:16,17**

## 8. Interaction makes people feel special.

Everyone wants to stay around someone who makes him or her feel special. Nobody wants to be a number or a statistic. Make your people feel special and they will stick to you like superglue!

# Chapter 45

# How to Interact with People

**1. Make a conscious decision to interact with people you do not know.**

It is not easy to talk to total strangers. We naturally gravitate towards things we know. In every man is the fear of the unknown. This makes us reserved and overly cautious. Break out and allow the rivers of living waters that are in you to bless humanity.

**2. Decide to do deep-sea fishing.**

Deep-sea fishing involves going into the midst of the large crowd and interacting with total strangers. You can do it! Decide to talk to five total strangers every Sunday. All pastors and leaders must be involved in talking to total strangers after each service. This will lead to the church growth we have been praying for.

**3. Show a genuine interest in the people who come to church.**

Do not look like an official of the church who is just doing a duty. Do away with fake smiles and decide to be genuinely interested in the people.

**4. Have a friendly smiling face.**

**A man that hath friends must show himself friendly...**
**Proverbs 18:24**

Practise smiling in front of your mirror. Some people have naturally stern faces; these ones need to practise smiling the most.

**5. Kill the spirit of hypocrisy by interacting with all kinds of people.**

Hypocrisy leaves a nasty taste in the mouths of everyone. Avoid it at all costs! Do not only ask for the names of wealthy looking people. Be genuinely interested in people who look poor and uneducated. Jesus interacted with every kind of person. He spoke to tax collectors, Pharisees, Centurions, fishermen, blind men, mothers, noblemen and even the dead!

> **My brethren, have not the faith of our Lord Jesus Christ, the Lord of glory, with respect of persons. For if there come unto your assembly a man with a gold ring, in goodly apparel, and there come in also a poor man in vile raiment; And ye have respect to him that weareth the gay clothing, and say unto him, Sit thou here in a good place; and say to the poor, Stand thou there, or sit here under my footstool: Are ye not then partial in yourselves, and are become judges of evil thoughts?**
> **James 2:1-4**

6. **Ask the seven basic interaction questions:**

==>Ask people what their names are.

==>Ask where they live.

==>Ask people where they work

==>Ask people where they attend school

==>Ask people whether they are married or getting married soon

==>Ask people whether they are committed to the church

==>Ask if you could be their friend.

## Chapter 46

# Eight Ways You Can Make People Feel Special

1.  **You can make people feel special by calling them by their names.**

When you call people by their names they feel special. They think to themselves, "The pastor knows me. I am one of the few people whose names he remembers. I must be one of the special few."

2.  **You can make people feel special by smiling at them and looking at them in the eye.**

Some faces are "smile-less". Some people naturally have a *serious* disposition. This *serious* look can be misread to be unfriendliness. If you are one such person, I repeat that you must practise smiling in front of your mirror. I had to do that! Ask your colleagues to help you to remember to smile. I asked my wife to help me to be friendly and she did!

3.  **You can make people feel special by being sincere and not exaggerating with them.**

When you flatter people, they tend not to take you seriously. At a point, people will think that you are scoffing at them. They may even curse you in their minds. When you say genuine things, no one will take you seriously anymore. If you want people to believe your compliments, you must learn to say what you mean and mean what you say!

**He that saith unto the wicked, Thou art righteous; him shall the people curse...**

**Proverbs 24:24**

## 4. You can make people feel special by looking for good qualities in them.

Everyone has good and bad qualities. If you want to build a meaningful relationship with anyone you must focus on the good things in the person. As you go along, you may have the opportunity to address real problems. Always remember this: if God were to address all your bad qualities on a daily or hourly basis, you would probably give up! That is why God changes us slowly as the months and years roll by. Be like God and acknowledge peoples' strong points. There will be a time to address shortcomings.

**That the communication of thy faith may become effectual by the ACKNOWLEDGING OF EVERY GOOD THING which is in you in Christ Jesus.**
**Philemon 1:6**

This verse *does not say* that our faith becomes effective as we acknowledge our sins! Our sins are before us everyday. Most people don't need anyone to remind them of their failures. This verse tells us that our faith becomes effective as we acknowledge good things and not bad things.

## 5. You can make people feel special by giving general compliments - it makes them feel good.

Say things like this:

- *I'm always glad to see you.*
- *I always thank God for your life.*
- *You are a real blessing.*

General compliments make people happy. People do not know why they are happy when they are complimented! Happiness just wells up within them. But make sure that you do not exaggerate or flatter anyone. Be genuine and you will always be taken seriously.

## 6. You can make people feel special by complimenting them about specific things-it makes them repeat their good deeds.

For instance, you could compliment people specifically like this:

- *I'm impressed with the way you come to church early.*
- *I like the way you pray fervently.*
- *You look very smart.*

When you compliment people about specific things, they are so happy that *they unconsciously decide to repeat that particular action.*

## 7. You can make people feel special by complimenting them in front of others.

When you say nice things about someone in front of other people, it adds more spice to the compliment. No one can buy a special compliment at the supermarket! When a pastor or church leader gives a compliment to a member, he is doing something that no one else can.

## 8. You can make people feel special by complimenting them at meetings.

When you compliment people in front of their colleagues, they feel rewarded for their hard work. The people we are trying hardest to impress are our peers! This is a fact of life. Many people are doing things just because their friends and colleagues are doing them. By complimenting somebody in front of his peers, you are putting a feather in his cap. Surely, this person will gravitate to you without even knowing why.

*Chapter 47*

# How to Encourage Interaction between Church Members

Interaction between church members is one of the most important keys to church growth. Not only must the pastor interact with the members, but the members must interact with each other.

## Six Steps to Encouraging Interaction between Church Members

### 1. Encourage the congregation to speak to one another in the service!

Do not dismiss the church service without encouraging members to say hello to each other. I often jokingly tell the members to say to each other, "I want to come home with you today for lunch." Sometimes I ask them to say to each other, "Are you married? Have you considered marrying me?" This makes everyone laugh but it loosens the atmosphere and encourages interaction.

### 2. Organize church camps and social events that make church members interact with each other.

Camps are one of the best forums for interaction. People are relaxed and get to know each other in an informal setting.

**And they, continuing daily with one accord in the temple, and breaking bread from house to house...**

**Acts 2:46**

### 3. Encourage church members to marry each other.

Let the church members know that the kind of person they want to marry can be found within the congregation. Once the church members begin to intermarry, you will have more stability in the church.

## 4. Encourage the church members to employ other church members.

**Neither was there any among them that lacked...**

**Acts 4:34**

The relationships within the church become deeper as the interaction goes deeper. Employers and employees sit together under the same pastor. Every large church has lots of members interrelating and interacting. It is this myriad of relationships that helps to stabilize the congregation!

## 5. Encourage your church members to support each other in times of celebration and mourning.

Let the church members know that it is their duty to participate in the events of others. You must realize that people will do what you tell them and they will believe what you say. This is a biblical instruction

**Rejoice with them that do rejoice, and weep with them that weep.**

**Romans 12:15**

## 6. Encourage the church members to make friends and to invite each other to their homes.

**And ALL THAT BELIEVED WERE TOGETHER, and had all things common.**

**Acts 2:44**

Once people have friends in the congregation, they will be glued to the church. Leaving the church becomes a little more complicated. Leaving the church now means leaving all your friends. Interaction between church members is truly a key to stabilising the congregation and encouraging church growth.

# Chapter 48

# P.V.T.I.

I have shared with you four main areas of a pastor's ministry. Prayer, Visitation, Teaching and Interaction (P.V.T.I.). It is my prayer that you will meditate on these things and apply them in your ministry.

Remember the code P.V.T.I., and you will always know what to do in the ministry. I pray that you will not replace the gold in the temple with brass. Stay with real ministry and you will have your reward from God in heaven. Do not try to please men. Avoid a 'pseudo ministry'! It is God who called you, and it is He you must seek to please!

May the Lord give you the desires of your heart as you fulfil your ministry. I believe that you will experience good success in your ministry as you put in practise these four great keys for church growth: *Prayer, Visitation, Teaching and Interaction!*